The Crows and The Train

By

K.B.

The Crows and The Train

Copyright © 2024 by Kat Bevins

Published by: Amazon Creative Hub
www.Amazoncreativehub.com

Table of Contents

The Man from Room #47 2
The Fire at the Psyche Ward 6
A New Home 19
A Call from Hell 25
A Call from Heaven 34
Midnight Sermons 38
A New World 50
A Walk With Thy Mentor 56
The Iron Beast 60
The Lesson of Faith and Life 66
Inside the Great Locomotive 72
The Frosted Stop 82
Finding Flames of Thee 89
The Schoolhouse 95
The Snow Will Melt 102
Missing Confrontations 108
Her Concierto 120
The Charring 132
The Encore 138
The Story Behind the Story 149

To The Sheep With The Softest Wool

The Man from Room #47

What is Hell?

It is a peculiar concept that causes many people to take different sides, for some think of it as a place that the damned deserve to go and rot, some think of it as a state of being, and others think of it as nothing more than a story to keep their children at bay.

As for me, I would not have thought that my opinion would matter; **Hell told me so.**

I had been kept a prisoner in Hell for quite some time, and it had resulted in my own mindscape leaving me. Without a mind to a body, my soul was tossed into a husk called, "The Man from Room #47."

I never chose that title, or received it as a gift, but it was wistfully forced upon me due to my lack of cooperation in Hell. The Man from Room #47 was a lulled man, and was constrained to bear a life of solitude. It was impossible to reconcile what I had done to deserve such Hell, for what once was my name had been warped into forgotten memories of my past. I was the Man from Room #47, and nothing past my memories of awaking in flames were coherent. I felt abandoned in this world, if there was even one left.

Inside of Hell, there was not a singular crimson flame in sight within my confinements of Room #47, but rather within the spitting tongues of the ones who kept the gates closed. They fed on the disgusting slop left behind by the despair of others, and they forced others to feed upon the misery as well. For me, they subjected my poor mouth to feed on false remedies. Bewilderingly enough, other men in rooms enjoyed the taste; they were allowed to keep their names because of the commitment. Whether they enjoyed the slop for malicious reasons, or to simply fit in, would always and forever be unknown, for it was more dangerous to speak one's mind than it was to simply enjoy a meal. My meals that the demons fed me had an end purpose, and besides destroying my pitiful mind, it was to lose all faith in ever escaping the gates.

One may ask where and what my faith belonged to, but I can no longer recall its origins. My lulled senses, which were bound to me through pitiful rations, have reconciled and dealt with any previous notion of a healthy life. Faith in myself was not in the equation at all, for the ability to even think was blocked by the feeding of demons. Faith, if had any, should be placed in something or someone else; a figure that one can trust will not succumb to those crimson flames. I would have wished upon any cloud out of Hell to let my faith float upon, but there was no creation for me to trust it should linger.

Everyone was condemned to Hell for a reason, and as for the Man from Room #47, I had a reason, just like the previous 46 rooms. However, my relentless resistance to feast on slop had caused me to forget the reason. I often questioned my acumen as to why I was in Hell, if it was not to learn from my condemnation. Why was I needed to be the Man from Room #47, if I did not recall why I was even in such a numbered room? I could not control the lulled senses, for they worked against me; everything had worked against me in an overwhelming notion of hopelessness.

I had lived a life of solitude for an unknown span of moments, even in my mind. When the solitude overcame my senses, and I was taken to the lulled mindset of the Man from Room #47, a great fog appeared to cloud my judgement. The fog was so thick that I had to cease all thoughts and await the clearing, but there would never be a clearing, as long as I was the Man from Room #47. However, with fog, there would appear a blank, white canvas for my mind to paint, never minding the notion of being watched. Making a purpose with what little was left, I created pictures of crows within my canvas, with the darkened beauties always watching me. The flock could freely fly in and out of the fog, seemingly only there to observe my story.

When not in the fog, my moments in Hell consisted of the same feasts and camaraderies. I would be awakened by the sound of rattling chains on my chest, as doors would open and close, appearing two demons in black and white outfits. They tormented me with conversation and false remedies for moments without an end, before finally fading away. What created Hell from their visit was the notion of conversing; shadows of the fog, neither me nor crows, screamed maliciously at us all. One either screamed back, or awaited the echoes to take their voice instead.

When there were moments of true clarity, inside my mindscape was a void of deafening silence, and at times, I had to return there to escape the screams of others. It was hard to know where my body went when the void consumed me, but it could not have gone too far, I assumed. The chains of salvation that were just out of reach had invariably reminded me of that. What used to be respectable locks of brown hair upon my scalp had morphed into a ragged, tangled, strangled piece of a crow's nest. It was long enough to tie a noose that would have ended my suffering, but, alas, one was not allowed to bring salvation unto oneself.

Room #47 was sturdier than the man within it. Pure stones and bricks made a prison with a small bed and slop bucket inside. Rats had never made it in, but I doubt they would have wanted to stay with me. The only thing to consistently stay by my side was the forest outside my gated window. No matter Night or Day, the sky teased freedom directly in my face.

It was not that I wished to stay in Hell, for I aspired to go beyond the fog. Unfortunately, I knew nothing past the canvas any more. That blur of blanc mists scattered with crows had become my physicality, mentality, and had now become my spiritual sense as well. The question lingered in my head: was I to choke on fresh air that I was no longer familiar with, or breathe in the flames that my body was no stranger to? I had faith in neither Heaven nor Hell, so I let the courses of the fog decide for me; maybe the fiery flames of Hell would not choke her out alongside me.

On that particular night, I had chosen to lie awake within my chamber, thinking of the fog and the crows once more, as my ignorance almost seemed to die off. Hell seemed to burn a little less that night, for the flames seemed to be elsewhere. Clouds of smoke materialised above my head; perhaps I could rest my faith upon those? Only when my mind fully cleared would my eyes shut entirely, tired from persistent blinking out of fear, and an urge to keep conscious. I beckon thee, no matter how hot the flames are, or how many crows watch thy story, **one must always keep conscious.**

The Fire at the Psyche Ward

It seemed that the most difficult part of my life was when the day left the night to watch me suffer. Thanks to Hell, neither Day nor Night was my friend, and neither did anything to help me. Unfortunately for both me and the crows, Night was always worse, for my aching body was in enough pain from the day, but those black and white demons were just getting started. I was forced to survive Day by demons that constantly kept me awake, but after the necessity of rest caught up, Night's demons would only work against my own two eyelids, and the will to stay awake. As much as I wanted a blissful slumber, I knew that if I fell asleep, the dark would consume me whole.

It was always the progressional weight of my eyelids that signified Night. As my range of vision ever so slightly lessened, I seemingly began to see more. The darkness became a portal for monsters to only be seen through a lens of unconsciousness. For the sake of my own half-dead being, I fought the lens until it fully opened, causing my eyelids to uncontrollably shut. The last moments of consciousness always felt guilty and defeated, like I deserved that Hell due to my eyelids' submission. Once my vision completely ceased, and I was forced to see the creatures of Night's Hell, it became a game to the demons of what would make me lose unconsciousness. Would it be the horrors of Hell, or a foreign entity taking pity on me? Through monstrous creations that lurked in Night's shadows, it was simply fear that drove the consciousness out of my mindscape. If not frightened to the astral plane, through a blistered dreamscape that I called my own would grant wishes of a peaceful, temporary death that was called slumber. Regardless of the two endings to the game, the house always seemed to win, as Day came back to continue the torture with a fresh start.

As one particular night seemed to follow the same pattern of depravity, I was awake in my chamber, and watched the crows outside my forbidden window. As they seemingly began to blend into the sky, the spawns of Hell lurked out of the corners of my vision. Each claw and set of teeth slowly invaded my entire line of sight, furthering my dismay, and the will to want my consciousness to end, for it seemed that hidden in the fog was where I was most at ease. While each creature taunted me for such a pitiful escape route, I found myself longing for relief once more.

One creature stood out to me, as they mocked my chains of life. Out of all of the times I had endured Hell, there was one demon that never missed a night of festivities. Like an unrestful corpse, what could be deemed as its skin was dehydrated and ruined with rips and cracks. Bleached colours contrasted its draining black hair, and used what could barely even be deemed as locks as a cover for its body. As if it were a draining parasite, it had no other intentions other than to haunt me.

Its mannerisms seemed as if they knew me like I knew the decrepit ribs easily seen through my chest. It twitched and smiled above me, bending over to get a better look at my chains and health-deprived state of being. When it appeared to grow closer, the other forms of darkness faded away, and joined the main centrepiece with murderous intentions. Even though the darkness ruined my vision, I could still see the reflections of the moonlight on its yellow, jagged teeth. Like a shooting star, I was falling down and losing my light very quickly, as I slipped further away from the sun.

That horror, if one could even call it that, seeing me as some sort of companion, was beyond what my nerves could take. Fear was an old friend that brought along new relations to meet my nerves, and needless to say, the door was regrettably opened. The rattling of my chains was apparent for the both of us that increased with shivers of terror and a newfound sense of blood running cold. Something compelled me to keep focus on the creature, for it was my mindscape knowing that to consume its poison would let me pass unto the night. Its hair met with gravity, as it pulled the disgusting locks down into my face, brushing my nose with a feeling of twine and thorns.

It was a great price to pay to be let into slumber, for the terrors of that creature met the highest bid for my insanity. The cold room felt stale, until the foreign entity materialised to seek pleasure in my torment. Any fear I had felt before could crumble before its suffocating breath. It knew the grip it possessed on my consciousness, and it knew that there were no other bidders. In a sharpening sight of fog, I noticed one thing about the entity that stood out from everything else, and it was its **eyes.**

The eyes looked like scribbles in a drawing of a child, an ink splatter on a doctor's note, or even the buttons of a scarecrow. It was the eyes that finally snapped my poor self into a dreamscape. I felt myself lose consciousness from the pure terror and fear I bestowed from such a demon's orbs of void; they were ones I would certainly never forget. As my line of vision blurred from splotches of grey and intoxication, the entity seemed to not be finished with me just yet. Until my line of sight was just those disgusting warts of eyes, it waited for the moment to finally make a move onto my soul.

I watched in paralyzed horror as it blinked. A void of evil blinked at me, as its crusted skin slowly fluttered onto me from the newfound action! It fluttered all the way down to my eyes, slowly floating closer and closer, until it landed right on my glazed eye! It covered my line of vision completely, causing me to lose sight of the entity in whole. Even in the small moment where I couldn't see the creature, it moved with a forceful notion, knowing it would finally be able to murder me.

Although my skin bore chains, the simple flake from Hell allowed me to break such force upon me! I flinched at the feeling of ash in my eye, and it caused the paralysis to immediately cease, forcing an uncontrollable jolt out of my body!

I moved…

I was actually able to move….I moved in the frozen ice from Hell!

However, now it was a game of figure skating, as the player from Hell could see me as equal now. Not that it ever decided to play fair in the first instance, but rather a twist of difficulty. We both knew that the second round was about to begin, and my solo would be first. We planned our routines in the blink of a twitching eye, and much like commanders at war, we plotted and fired our attacks one right after the other. I was a graceful dancer, for I chose to not perform illegal tricks and moves against the ice.

I immediately spun along tracks that were left by the crows, and left the ice in mist. My only goal was to perform in hopes of spinning enough to create a fog, and then I knew it wouldn't be long until I could escape once more. The creature joined the rink in the distance, shortening my time in the spotlight. If I wanted to impress anyone, now would be my only chance to do so, before the returning champion took the rink. The question that separated me from the deceitful creature, was the notion of who we performed for.

I performed every act like it was my final for the audience. The creature performed for the judges to let them critique and glorify what damned Room #47. The fog was growing thicker against the clashing of our sharp skates, but one could always see the tattered demon's illegal turns and twists. It appeared that the audience didn't care much about the legality, as long as a show was put on. Dancing on that rink to save my life was a testimony to breaking paralysis, but it furthered my insanity from the demon's tricks.

Such a flaming entity spun on such a cold surface, however, the steam it emitted from such force finally created the proper fog I needed to escape. The only thing that stood in my way then, was how to fade into the fog without being followed. In order to escape, I would have to dance in order to leave the rink without a suspicious routine. The audience roared with anticipation, as I took one last final bow, before my final trick.

For the final trick, there was no ice skating rink, there were no dancers, or an audience watching. It was the Man from Room #47, chained to a wall, against a spawn from Hell wanting to harvest this soul. The notion of a trick was to impress a viewer with a rare and unsuspecting talent. What talent could the Man from Room #47 possibly have? It was then upon which I realised what I possessed that was so rare and unsuspecting, for it was an actual consciousness.

Regardless of what visions and creatures I saw, I knew not to submit unto any, despite their yelling to drown my consciousness. The shouting and cackling were never actual words, just screams of nonsensical gibberish. I began to see their ways to destroy my mindscape as failures, and with my consciousness cleared, I was able to truthfully perform on ice against them, instead of falling through. For my final trick, I looked at the spawn from Hell, and closed my eyes willingly. I refused to let fear or convulsions do it for me, but rather allowed a clear conscience to win the gold medal instead.

I could hear their screams once more, as many came out to sing and chant sounds of burning glass, but I would not let the fear consume me. I let my dreams restore the fog, as the crows mocked their screeching for me. The cries from the flames' consumption burnt out, as the fog stirred in full. In a final, fading moment, I was at peace, and for the first time, I had a little cup of faith. Not necessarily in myself, but rather the crows.

What once was just a mere comfort had finally come full circle, and had been transformed into a symbol of hope. During moments of consciousness, they have always flocked to me when I needed them the most, and now during the moments of most wanted times of Night as well. Never once had I called upon the crows, but their ominous, watchful presence was enough to ward off any thought of submission to full insanity. Thanks to their glowing eyes, I was able to enjoy the fog of bliss once more.

There was no feeling of chains here, or even a notion of captivity. It was a complete and absolute place of contentment with crows in the distance. I had the option of running, crying, waltzing, or screaming, but I always chose to just sit and admire the grey beauty.

Tonight was different. In honour of overpassing the ashes of Hell, I decided to lie down and look at the fog from below. Like clouds in the world outside, the fog would lightly float along into a blanket, which all came back to celebrate my consciousness. No one else, except the Man from Room #47, could enjoy the fog and the crows as much as I could. I laid there, and looked at everything against a voiding floor, just admiring the silent camaraderie of grey.

I felt my eyes finally grow heavy from all of the pleasant sensations, after hours of longingful daydreams. I eased into full slumber, as I felt no need to stay awake any longer. No dreams were present, but the notions of what made them sweet resided. I would remain in that state of bliss, until the crows awakened me. As per usual in a foggy dream, the crows awoke me from slumber, but I could tell that something was gravely false.

When I awoke from my daze, I noticed the murder leaving me. I couldn't understand why they'd leave me now, even through what we've shared together..

Perhaps they weren't leaving me, but urging me to follow them..

They flew with great intensity in a direction far away from anything I could conceivably gain from walking. As they faded into the fog, I stood to follow them, but quickly realised that I would need to run if I ever wanted the chance to see them again.

With each running step, I noticed my eyes began to burn, and wanted to shut out of instinct. The dreamful air became more surreal with each grip against my choking throat. Growing more difficult to move, I staggered in the deceitful, greying fog. That was not fog; that was smoke! The crows had left me, hoping I'd chase after them in my dulled senses to escape from the smoke!

Suffocating in my dreamscape, I began to force myself to wake up into the real world. With each painful gasp for air, I found each sense coming back into reality. Finally, I made it back to Hell, but not without feeling the effects of smoke filling my body. I coughed and wheezed for exasperating moments, convulsing and shaking against Hell itself. There were no creatures here, for the smoke was something not even a native could bear, for it felt like it was something purposefully planned like a child's runaway trick.

I needed to escape that pit, before I was consumed by the hole of despair. Feeling the chains' nails that pierced into my skin, I turned around the best I could to fight their grasp. I grabbed the hot chains that were bolted to the wall, and with the utmost strength I could materialise, I pulled harshly against the interlocking iron circles. I burned my hands from touching the chains of Hell, and it immediately caused me to let go in between screams. There was not a singular effect on the rusted chains, for their grip seemed to outlast death itself.

I knew that if I did not escape their clutches, I would soon join death as well. I yanked and lashed away from the cuffs, but it was no use. Hell was using flames to make me look like I truly belonged to the title, The Man from Room #47. That place had all intentions of keeping me from escaping, regardless of any scream or squawk from a dying crow.

Everything possible had left the blaze now, all except for me, my blistered hands, and my choked lungs. My eyes watered with tears, fear, and anger, as the crushing notion overcame me. I knew that I was going to die alone, just like any other damned soul in here. Nothing was here to help me anymore, and I began to lose hope in helping myself. The sounds of my chains' strained screams seemed to die out, as I regrettably replaced theirs.

Inside of Hell, there were nothing but flames, monsters, and evil notions ready to make one join the camaraderie. In between my cries of dismay, I grew closer to accepting the final punishment. Remembering all of my life, as it flashed before my eyes, I could think of nothing but deceitful trickery bestowed upon me. The only thing that offered peace to my flesh were my crows, but now they've escaped the torment. I wanted to join the crows, more than anything else, whether it be through death or a sudden work outside of Hell.

Both options seemed to be unlikely for such a wretched soul of mine, for even if I was an innocent man, the title of the Man from Room #47 robbed me of that liberty. I had been damned to that place, and it had caused me those final moments of suffering. I closed my eyes for a moment of clarity, but saw only smoke. Hell would allow death, but never with a blissful moment of peace, even in the moments leading to the final verse. While my voice strained with nothing blissful to sing, I simply wished for the chorus to play out.

I cried the chorus louder than a fortississimo, as the requiem seemed to accompany my dynamics. I didn't know who I sang for anymore, for myself didn't even seem worthy. Perhaps it was a cry to the crows, or simply anything outside of Hell.

May my voice haunt thee whoever heard the damnation of a wretched, unjust conviction.

However,

it seemed my voice did reach feathers above,

for the chorus had reached a key change.

The next beat was conducted by a distinct snap from the chain, quickly falling to the bed. More snaps and crackles were heard, as I wasted no time to get up from the mattress. So many thoughts ran faster than I did, with a direct result of the smoke that completely filled the room. The rush to the door caused me to fall to my knees, scraping them against the cold stone. Adrenaline carrying me, I fought against my eyes that were lost to unfocused vision, all while I rushed to make it back towards the door.

Although the crows were gone and the creatures were down under, I knew they were all together, waiting for me to come through the smoke. At that moment, I felt nothing but overwhelming urges to get back up, despite my body wanting to linger there. I knew the only matter of survival would be to give up my body, and let my soul run free, no matter where, or even if it made it out. Conducting at a faster tempo, I left my body as I got up, and pushed through the smoke; the door coming down with it.

The Man from Room #47 wouldn't have been able to push down a door with ease, the Man from Room #47 would not have been able to break the chains that bound him there, but most importantly, the Man from Room #47 would not have been able to accept help from the crows outside. I was no longer the Man from Room #47, but rather a merely trapped soul escaping back to the murder of crows. No longer being able to see, I let my soul travel through the labyrinth of flames, as each limb of my body seemed to fight against it. My throat screamed and lashed at myself, with each and every stab of the flames against my feet and fingers. The puncture wounds slowly travelled up my body, as the fabric of my clothes caught amongst the eternal blade.

I couldn't focus on the pain that my body was materialising, for the focus needed to be on how to escape these foreign walls, now being eaten alive by Hell. I couldn't focus on the notions of these stone walls being caught on fire, but rather how I wouldn't be caught as well. Whether I was mad or not no longer mattered, for that was the Man in Room #47's problem. These stone walls were on fire, and so would I, if I did not leave that anguish immediately. With my entire world seemingly collapsing behind me, I cried out, hoping my tears might even extinguish the flames that clutched onto my skin, as it all seemed to move faster.

I turned down a hallway, and was immediately greeted with a full blaze of ambering teeth. I had no time to make the decision whether to turn back or not, for that decision was made by my soul following the murder. Fully seeing Hell's reign, I realised that I was leaving the gates of such a place! It was no wonder that every creature of Hell left me, for they were all here now, guarding the exit. No matter the feeling of my skin melting off of my own body, or the drugged dread of when looking forward to a smoke-filled painting of Hell's horrors, I preserved out of the gates.

With a final notion of screams from every single party, including the creatures, murder, and mine, I made it out of the blaze! However, it was not done in a clean, singular cut, but with three stinging lashes against my back. It flung me forward onto the ground, just out of the flame's reach. Almost like a spoiled child, Hell picked what meat it liked off of my skeleton, and then proceeded to spit me out like I was nothing. I lifted my head slowly up from the ground, quietly beginning to comprehend that I had joined the murder outside.

Tiny blades of dead grass prickled under my skin. It itched, as its brown, greenish colours tickled my forearms and knees. I slowly looked up, and before me laid a hill downwards to the town. I was no longer looking at the forced fixture of nature, but civilization in itself! The small silhouettes of buildings were far, but still so much closer than Hell ever offered.

Above the silhouetted buildings were a line of trees and valley tops; all too dark to truly admire. Beyond the line of nature was a thick pool of darkness, with fishes of light about. It seemed that the fish had no source of true food, but derived it from worship of the bobber. Much like my own scales, I could now fully see the ocean in its full azure void. Finally escaping the tangled reef, the flow of the wind gently brushed against my arms.

The wave was powerful, not in strength, but in voice. From the bottom of the ocean, I could see how little I was compared to the bobber. All of the other ocean dwellers, whether they noticed the source or not, could not overthrow these waves. The waving wind welcomed me into the new world, despite my lack of experience from the previous. I looked up to see where the murder had gone, and saw that they had flocked to the ocean's bobber.

From that moment, I was forever in debt to **the great big moon in the sky**, and the mother of nature that tried its best to comfort me.

A tear rolled down my cheek in realisation that this was my saviour, and this was who the murder followed. From the grace of the moon, my gashes seemed to cool off with the cold night air, but I knew the breeze would not last forever. It would stay long enough for its breath to guide me to a new place. From my previous cage of Hell, I learned that following myself only led me to myself, so the choice of the moon's breath was optimal. Letting it fill me with strength, I slowly came off the grass, and unto my feet.

The numbing sound of the night sky no longer muffled the sounds of burning ash from my new point of life. The heat behind my back whispered profanities towards my new being, trying to make me lash out in strife. The breeze fought against the smoke to save my ridges of burned flesh, keeping me from falling back. In truth, I felt a small push forward. **The great big moon in the sky** was calling me to my new world, and to let go while I still could, knowing I would grow fearful of Hell's return if I didn't start walking.

My first step forward consisted of my head spinning lightly. Both of my eyes scouted the newfound charts of land, like a hummingbird for nectar. My second step met up with my first, and calmed my nerves back down, like a resting squirrel in hibernation. Settling among the breeze, however, reached my body's sense of touch. The prickly grass now scratched ever so lightly at my cliffs of skin, and seemed to beckon the rivers of blood back.

Why was **the great big moon in the sky** doing this to me? Though what I once thought was an act of deceit with false notions of trust, I now realised it was to keep me going; I was not allowed to dwell. My third step happened subconsciously, whether from pushing pin needles into my feet, or hoping for dulled ones in the next. The grass and the breeze danced among me, and it sharpened, yet dulled my senses all at the same time. Never once did I feel completely alive; that was until I looked up at the moon. Gazing up at my guide once more, I felt both notions entirely at once.

With my eyes readjusting to the orb of light, my body followed in its command. Steps along the grass away from Hell no longer felt like walking, but rather a floating waltz. I was among the stars in the sky, as I let the breeze carry what was left. The crows seemed to follow my mentor as well, for we all waltzed unto the quiet town before us, never caring of Hell, or any scribbled orbs following.

In a straight, careless line, I danced with the moon and its crows down the hill, and into the neighbourhood of sleeping houses. I did not once take my eyes off of my partner, not even to gaze at the foreign architecture. I never paid attention to the bumpy, worn cobblestone roads, or the roofs made with moonlight shingles. Each window had small candles lit within them, but I refused to let them avert my waltz. Their twinkling fire was no match for the burning brights that were the stars. Noises of crickets, and blowing winds filled the streets, as well as my soul.

The small fires harnessed by wax behind glass seemed to slowly dim out, while I furthered deeper into town. I felt as if the moon was telling me something; I was higher than fire. It didn't quite make sense to me at the time, but I knew that the answer would be revealed by the end of the night. Putting my faith above once more, I continued to waltz higher than the candles' flames. The heat from the fire and its smoky breath no longer crept alongside my shadows from the moonlight, for I was finally guided safely away from Hell. My gaze was so interlocked with my mentor's, that I did not even see the cloud forthcoming to blanket the moon. With one final breath, our waltz finally ended.

No longer in contact with my mentor, I looked down at the town before me, and saw where the moon had taken my soul. Standing tall, yet at ease, was a structure with an aura of notions I could not put into words just yet.

My body chilled at the sight, my eyes went in and out of focus with each breath of mine it stole, and my knees grew weak with an utter collapse. Furthering my gaze unto the colossal building, what struck me were the windows. They seemed cracked, yet unbroken; a rainbow, but one solid hue; stained yet pure; oh how the windows sang without a flame to shine. The picture they formed was not yet shown, for no light gave it a voice. Still, the power in its silence was louder than any flame.

The doors it bestowed were two crimson doors, with black handles in shapes of perfect circles. They so perfectly contrasted the black frame outside, yet matched in tone of voice. The place was all so welcoming, regardless of the flames or night; I even felt welcomed as myself, and not as the poor Man from Room #47. I was thankful for the moon's introduction of the mysterious building, and the crows that followed me here, for I knew Hell could never follow me into such a place. Some of the black feathered beings sat perched upon the steep roofing, beckoning me to go inside.

I knew the moon had brought me here for a reason, but I still questioned the right to enter. My knees seemingly lifted on their own, enduring the sickening pains from scrapes, gashes, burns, and cuts. The breeze was blocked by the building, leaving no choice but to gently push me into its arms. I gave into the night wind, and walked to the doorstep of the building. It was in that moment of bliss that I decided that if I ever encountered another wretched soul like mine, it would be my duty under the great big moon in the sky to help them follow the crows to freedom, like I had just achieved. I beckon thee, one must always **pursue the next step, no matter the risk.**

A New Home

I placed my charred hand against the crimson door with feelings of doubt. I felt so unworthy to even stand near this building, but, alas, I was the Man from Room #47 no more; I was worthy of feeling. I knocked on the door, trying not to sound like the fiends from Hell that used to bang on Room #47's door, regardless of my consent to open it. I felt ashamed in knocking, for I planned to still open it, but I had to remember that the moon allowed me to open it, and not the Man from Room #47. With a gentle push among the doors, they opened with ease.

The wave of a new breeze pulled me in, as shut the doors behind me. Inside was a whole new realm of darkness. Unlike Hell, the void provided comfort; it was something my soul deserved. The cold air within the building numbed every single gash and burn upon my flesh, almost like they were healing from the comfort within. The place echoed from the tall ceilings, with my feet shuffling among the smooth floors of pure stone.

Low ambient tones seemed to echo back to me, like a call to move forward. Surrounded by deafening darkness, it would truly be an act of faith to progress. Looking above where I knew my mentor was, I walked with my eyes drawn to the void up high. As if I had called for the moon to return, the place was suddenly lit with auras and beams of light like no other. Peeking through the stained glass was my mentor!

The moon shined through the head window far ahead of me, allowing me to finally see the building's mysterious figure in truth. Illuminated by the moon's multiple colours from the glass ahead, rows of flattened benches were facing forward, each with oak wood and perfectly rounded edges of boards. The end of the building was elevated, with a main piece of wood in the centre. Alongside the back laid crosses and floral arrangements guarded by notions of endearment. While hard to make out the true colours and types of flowers, they were still beautiful under the moon's gaze.

Thanking the moon once more, I looked into its eyes directly. To my surprise, I was instead greeted with the eyes of a murder perched along the window seal. They squawked and flapped, like they were insisting I came closer. Following my mentor's advice once more, I walked closer to the back. Closing in on the furthest wall, I could see something to the far right, barely touching the corner.

While hard to see, I noticed a border along the wall of a different hue. The door-shaped shadow seemed to be much darker in colour than its neighbouring greyed walls. As I walked to the darkened door, I felt a stronger sense of what this place embodied. Knocking on the door, it opened without me trying the knob. This room welcomed me in, somehow more than what the building itself gave already.

The room was warm with reminiscent notions of peace and tranquillity. The wood seemed more relaxed, and the curtains within seemed more at ease. Laid before me was a small room, seemingly someone's resting chambers. Near the door was a desk, and a wardrobe against the opposite wall. Next to the wardrobe was a bed with an alluring painting overhead.

Between the bed and the desk was another door; one I dared not to enter just yet, for I felt my body's pleas for rest growing more apparent by the moment. Across the door was the curtained window. The curtains and the bed's linen seemed to match with deep crimson and pure white tones. Everything within the room had a perfect balance of black and white, even in the small moments of darkness. The painting was what pulled the room together, in my opinion; it was of a frosted pond with crows visiting in the bare trees.

Pulling back the curtain gently, I was greeted with the beautiful night sky upon me. My mentor was still in view, and even welcomed me inside of the new room. I was confused as to why this room was revealed to me, for it had to belong to someone else. Turning around once more to face the room, I opened the wardrobe to find a better image of who this room belonged to. Beyond a thin layer of dust rested a coat hung on a wire, a hat on the top shelf, and a mask.

The familiar, foreign feeling of what this place bestowed grew stronger, as I looked at the three mysterious items. I took the coat out of the wardrobe, and gently placed it on the bed. Getting a better look at the garment, I noticed the length and void of colour it had. The long, black, wool coat had a distinct beauty to it, and was further complimented by the small, crimson embroidery on the collar and cufflinks. While inspecting the lining, I noticed that the breast pocket had a name embroidered onto its lining: **Father Drexel.**

Reading those stitched words over and over materialised the utmost of the indescribable notion. I could tell from the moon that this was what my mentor wanted me to find. Many questions as to who this Father Drexel figure was dashed about in my head, yet I never danced with the answer. How was he a father, who was he the father of, where was he now, what did he do, and when will I encounter him?

I was intrigued, and the pursuit to find more guided me to his desk. I quickly turned to the father's desk, with somewhat of a feeling of urgency. I was even beginning to feel rushed to learn more! I bent over and looked at the wooden table with an assortment of candlesticks and papers. Even under the phasing moonlight, I could read the many letters and documents on Father Drexel's desk.

A stack of papers in the middle of the desk seemed to be letters to the man, while neighbouring ones surrounding the father's mail were documents of the building itself. The neighbours of letters revealed the name of the building; it was the Cathedral of something? In every document alongside the table were names scribbled out that would have given me the satisfaction of knowing the name of this place. Frustrated but still intrigued, I continued to look at the Cathedral of Mystery's papers. The documents led me nowhere but a variety of attendance, however, the letters in the middle that were seemingly written to the father of the cathedral painted the whole picture clear as the night sky.

"September 5th, 1518. Thy sermon was sensational! One could heareth cries of joy from the furthest pew! With preaching like such, thou could banish the plague o' danse. Speaking of such, I hope thy mission of healing spreadeth no bounds; a mission from God indeed your saving is."

"September 9th, 1518. I bring news to thee of an outbreak upon a few cousins in the cathedral. The refuge thy cousins sought in teachings has fully come in danse. I pleadeth thee to watch over thy glory of the cathedral, which will include thyself."

"September 12th, 1518. May God speed thy healing. Forever in Grace of the cathedral."

A cold shiver ran up my aching bones. What happened to the graceful Father Drexel? Was he struck by the plague, or did he escape it entirely? While searching for the answer, there was a sheet of paper crumpled up in the corner of the desk, seemingly discarded with solemn notions. Picking it up and unravelling the answer felt forbidden, but my mentor kept reassuring me that it was okay.

"September 10th, 1519. I am"

That was all that was written. The handwriting was not shaken, or even a slurred last letter. It was written in the utmost perfect handwriting; the ink even looked equal in all lines! Something about the unfinished sentence shook me to my core, for why would a father only proclaim that I am? Was he ran off from the final words, or did he disregard answering entirely?

I turned to my mentor for answers. Why was it that the moon revealed so much yet nothing? Gazing at the night sky, I was interrupted by a black flap of wings. A crow was now perched outside the window, returning the gaze I once gave to its home. With a solemn feeling, it politely asked me to open the window.

I couldn't refuse the creature, for the feeling of wanting to leave a place was no stranger to me, but also the feeling of wanting to come to the Cathedral of Night Dwellers was now a familiar custom as well. Opening the window for the crow, it flew inside and sat upright on the wired coat hanger. The crow was like a messenger from the moon, and I was an eager man to hear the word. Despite a lack of voice, we communicated through conversations. However, what the crow told me were words I did not believe.

Every time I asked as to why I was bestowed such a cathedral of fortune, it tilted its head and squawked at the crumpled paper, I am. Every time I asked as to what the ending of the letter was, it tilted its head and squawked at me, I am. Every time I asked as to what happened to Father Drexel, it tilted its head and squawked at me, I am. Every time I asked where the father was now, it tilted its head and squawked at me, I am. Every time I denied my being as the same of Father Drexel, it tilted its head and squawked at me, I am.

How could I possibly be Father Drexel? I was a man of no class, my time in Hell fought his time in Heaven, and I knew nothing of this cathedral! I wanted to lash out at the crow for being so insistent on a falsehood, but then I thought of the other eye. Perchance, it was not my previous role before Hell, but rather the new role I must fulfil. The Man from Room #47 becomes Father Drexel.

I looked at the crow once more with new pupils, before making my final decision. I left my previous life so quickly and waltzed into another like it was nothing of such, that it didn't even feel real. The only way I knew that it wasn't a poor trick from Hell was the reassurance from my mentors. Both the moon and the crows worked to set me free and let me abide within the Cathedral of Homage, so that I felt it was okay to become a father. I knew that becoming Father Drexel meant a future of a person, rather than a nothing living in ash and faecal matter.

People needed Father Drexel, and I was willing to fulfil the need. I believe I was destined to be the father of this cathedral, and I would continue to keep the name pure. Turning to the crow, I wanted to make a vow to it, but it had already vanished into the night. A small sigh escaped me, as I stuck my head out of the window, feeling the night breeze once more. Looking up to the moon, I cried out for the first time in a long while.

"I accept thou as my mentor, and shall follow thy guide! Now I serve unto thee for others to learn as well! Praise to thee, o' Gracious Moon!"

My voice seemed to echo unto the night sky, and summon the murder to fly onto the roof. The moon seemed warmer, and so did my fleshed bones. Feeling the final moment of clarity washing over, and tiring my body to the point of collapsing, I gently shut the window once more, and hung the coat back up into the wardrobe. It was my coat now, and my crumpled paper, I am. Rest shortly overtook me, causing my collision with the bed.

Stings of pain hurt my person, as my back met with the bed, but I tried to pay no mind to them; my mentor would let it all work out. I rolled over into the sheets, rested my head onto the pillow, and closed my eyes in relief. The moon seemed to dim for me, allowing my eyes to finally rest. I will admit, my emotions got the better of me in a moment of gratitude and acceptance, and left puddles in the sheets, but I felt comforted within each tear in a sense of ease. It was okay to cry, for the great big moon in the sky thought of tears as the birth of acceptance.

I cried until I completely washed away my consciousness, and let my dreamscape float ashore. I used to fear sleeping, but I no longer worried, now that I was representing Father Drexel; Hell could not burn a man under the moonlight. Through a new person must also materialise new dreams, yes? I was ready to accept the father's dreamscape, no matter how different it may be, with or without the bliss of the fog. I beckon thee, one must always **be ready to accept a new role when called upon.**

A Call from Hell

Falling into my new dreamscape, I landed among lulled cosmos that floated among my feet. There was not a single puff of fog, but rather a whole collection of nebulas ahead of me! I flew among stars, furthering my embodiment into Father Drexel. Feeling no pain among the dreamy sky, I only thought of how a man dreams as such. Like dancing in complete waves of water, everything felt slow, but ever so free.

All I saw was a galaxy before me, different coloured stars twinkling in endless directions. It was such a blissful difference of dreams between my fog filled with a murder of crows and this danse of cosmos. One only could wonder if these dreams were what awakened his teachings. I knew that they would be my muse, for my teachings needed to bring the same wonder as these stars. White noise filled my ears, as the cold, yet warm atmosphere hugged my body.

There was a beauty in dreaming, and I was finally blessed by the moon to experience it.

Alas, I should have known it would not last forever, for Father Drexel wouldn't have abandoned his name with a dreamscape like this. Each star seemed to fade away slowly, almost at a pace I never noticed. The cosmos burned less and less until only a void surrounded me; not even I burned a glow. A seemingly endless darkness choked out the stars, as I landed on a wet, flat ground against something hard. I shivered slightly at the cold sensation, with each splash against my bare feet.

I began walking in the direction I had landed, for I trusted in the moon's placement for me. To walk in a seemingly endless path of nothing is a peculiar feeling, to say the least. It was not foreign to me, but I didn't appreciate the nerves it brought alongside it. There were no crows to comfort here in this dreamscape; just noir. I took small pity on the father, but at least his stars were like crows preparing him for the void.

The only question I had then was what the darkness meant. My fog of crows came from a want of tranquillity; a soul in need of rest. What did this world mean to Father Drexel, and how did he escape it? I wasn't confined to the Man from Room #47 anymore; I could change how the dreams were pruned. However, I needed to find a scent of creation within this destruction.

I kept walking down the endless void, levelling my head with each quiet splash; I was ready to find something foreign. I called out to my mentor with an echoing voice, choked by a black hole, to grant me a vision. The darkness was now the moon's canvas. I was willing to study any portrait, whether it would be Heaven or Hell. For the Cathedral of Dreams' sake, I would endure anything the moon called to me.

The painter took its brush and dipped it in oil. Then, with a thunderous force, the painter flung its brush at the canvas, creating a small splat of oil. Compared to the rest of the black canvas, the oil made quite an impression. The oil just sat there, slowly running off the easel. As soon as it completely ran off, another splatter was added.

The moon granted my request, and granted me a vision alright, for a large explosion of sound shot from behind me. With the echoing dreamscape, the sound intensified in my eardrums, rattling my thoughts and mind. Nothing followed the shot of noise, except its echoing voice, but it felt as if it was following me at the time. When the echoes finally died, another one was fired, and it felt ever so closer to my ringing ears. These shots of explosions sounded like roaring cannons!

I will admit that I jumped at each fire, and it caused me to quicken my pace to try and outrun the noise. I never did wish to truly look behind me to see the source of the noise. Something told me that my mentor had not finished painting the source just yet, for it would be wrong to judge the unfinished piece.

The shots were growing louder, and so did the materialising smoke rings that formed behind me. They'd drift above my head, and disappear in the next blink. Even having faith, it was hard not to be fearful at times. When the heat of the shots fired began to ghost my head, I was told it was okay to look. Turning my head around to face the roaring explosions, I could undoubtedly see a cannon being pushed by an ominous figure.

The cannon was iron black with wheels of darkened steel. Pushing it ever so closer was a figure in a porcelain white cloak. With a hood covering my pursuer's face, it was hard to make out anything of character physically. However, no one could deny the atmosphere that walked among them. The opposite of the Cathedral of Bliss, salvation offered through the emptiness of a drugged mind, and a conscious thought that sleepwalked among others.

Was this white-cloaked figure the demon from Hell? As unnerving as it seemed, there was not a singular connection between the demon from Hell and the white-cloaked pursuer in my mindscape, for there was no way that tattered demon could possibly hide its face! They both radiated a sense of evil, but my pursuer's was heavily guarded with a mask of purity, from their appearance to their collected mannerisms. There was not a world where the tattered demon could ever mask their evil aura, and it would never fail to make me bend over from indescribable pain. The white-cloaked figure was something I could withstand, but it was still no stranger to that drugging notion.

I couldn't believe that the two were the same being, but I could believe that my pursuer was a descendent who was accustomed to purity.

I was not ready for a confrontation of this degree, for I had not fully learned the way of the father just yet. The pair of hidden eyes that pierced right through me were menacing in more ways than one could describe, and I could only fear they looked like scribbled voids. I couldn't bear the thought any longer; I turned back and began running away from my pursuer and their cannon to create a space of distance between us. It felt like they were aware of my existence in this realm, but couldn't quite see me, for I was their ghost of the haunted house. Scaring me so, the need for space was not enough.

We had a couple of metres between each other, but a cannon could easily clear that with smoke itself. I ran as fast as my astral legs could take me, and shot glances behind my back with every competing blow. My pursuer never did pick up pace, so the metres between us grew exponentially. With the echoes seemingly starting to quiet, I knew I would be safe, as long as my pursuer did not become fully conscious. A part of me was worried that I would alert the white-cloaked figure of my existence from the repeated splashes of water against my dashing feet, but it became clear that the puddles were no issue to either of us, or at least to my deafened ears that obnoxiously rang.

With every flinch I made from the fires, I seemed to grow less afraid of the cannons. Perhaps this was the goal of the moon? I believed that my mentor was preparing me for an ominous threat in the not-so-distant future, for the distance between me and the cannon might be the distance between me and my impending fight with my pursuer. Feeling a new wave of confidence, I gathered my spunk and continued running, seemingly invigorated. Splashes went up my legs less and less, as I picked up speed, almost as if I was flying; that was until I tripped over something harsh.

I felt a immediate pain in my foot, and with a hard splat into the water, I fell onto the foreign floor. I no longer cared about the cannon slowly travelling here, but instead cared about the cold iron that breached the surface of the water. Two colossal beams, parallel to each other, were about a metre and a half apart. Under the beams were pieces of horizontal wood, barely under the water. Was this a new style of road, or perhaps a foreign footpath?

I had the option to either cross or follow the iron footpath; I could stay here and let the cannon catch up, or I could continue the lesson of what my mentor was teaching. In the end, I took the iron footpath as a new way, and began to follow its trail. The cannon never seemed to change directions, and also never seemed to notice my new path. We had finally parted ways, but the sounds of the cannon never quite did. Something told me that my pursuer would find me one way or another, regardless of the new path.

Walking along the wood felt rough against my bare feet, but served as a nice change against the floor of the void. I questioned the importance of this footpath, and with my mentor seemingly reading my mind, I was granted another vision. In the distance, a sign seemed to materialise. Approaching it with mixes of eagerness and caution, I slowly studied each of the colours and symbols.

The sign's head was shaped like an X, and its face matched with black and white tones. Unintelligible words were written on each part of the cross, but I knew too well that it was in another language. What a strange sense it was to read words in a language one could never understand. They shared my alphabet, so why not my words? The sign kept its head quite high, or at least simply higher than mine, but never once did it mock me for my height.

I admired the sign, but was lost in further thought when I saw its arms. Two fairly large metallic circles were horizontally placed alongside its torso, with brims along a hollowed circle in the middle. I questioned the contents inside its circles, so with a moment of truth, I put my eye against the middle, and took a look inside. All was darkness, until a sudden noise of power hollered! It was an indescribable charge of power, but it led from the pole to the circles in the blink of an eye.

In the next flinch, I was blinded by pure beams of light, like the sun itself was on the other side. I fell back from the sudden shock, groaning from the strain put upon my eyes. My head hit the water, ever so close to the protruding iron beam beside me, for I would have been a dead man if I had landed any differently. Thanking my mentor once more, I let my eyes adjust to the new light. It was a blood-like colour that seemed to flow out of the rays, but upon further inspection, it was only one of the circles of light that radiated such crimson brightness.

I stood back up, my backside now completely drenched, and steadily examined the sign once more. As if on queue to my readiness, the cannon in the distance fired, finally catching me off guard once more. It seemed to be louder than what I remembered from the last conscious hearing of the fire, and it made me feel ever so more fearful. Was this sign a futuristic way of foreboding my demise from the cannons? I looked to see if I could see my pursuer in the distance, and to my horror, they were on the iron footpath, and ever so slowly moving faster!

I slowly began to panic more, for I did not know what to do with the sign just yet. I debated calling the moon for answers, but I felt that I was simply not seeing the full picture entirely. The white-cloaked figure was more apparent now, even behind the reddened gaze of the light. I decided it would be best to continue running, for it seemed that they had noticed my existence in full. Was it from my cries against the iron footpath?

I had no time to think further into the question of how, but only could afford to answer my own distress by leaving once more. I began to follow the red gaze of the sign down the iron footpath, quickening my step with each increasingly louder roar of the cannon. The ring of smoke entered my field of vision once more, as it floated above my head again. I would not let myself be subjected to the heat of the fire, and instead fled from the thunderous roar altogether. The echoing march of the cannon with its wheels grinding against the iron beams seemed to drive me insane to the point that it felt like I was hallucinating bell chimes!

These ominous bell chimes were faster than the elongated roars of the cannon, but were easily drowned out by the echoes. The distance of the bells made me question their authenticity, but then I had a ponderous question; was it from the sign? I turned around to see if the sign had changed in stature any, and to my surprise, the lights within the sign's circles were flashing; alternating if thou will. Without a doubt, those chimes were materialising from the sign, but for what reasons did they scream so hard to reach me? My question was finally answered, but not by the notions of the moon, but something foreign.

Behind my body was a mellifluous cry that invoked far more power than the bell chimes or the cannon. I immediately fell to my knees at the multiphonic shrill that sent shivers of mystery up my person, and splashed into the water between the two iron beams. All was silent except for the chimes, for they grew louder from the empowering crescendos of the seemingly automaton voice. I turned around in the direction of the haunting whistle, refusing to stand out of the water. What my eyes landed upon was a blanket of thin darkness slowly unveiling itself to be an autonomous creation of horror.

With another shrill of pure haunting harmonies, it revealed its mysterious face to my strained and fearful eyes. A beacon of a pure golden glow was focused from its pupils, as its smoky hair began to grow in puffs. It gritted its teeth at me, while breathing out against flying water. Approaching me slowly was a colossal iron beast, huffing and screaming with increasing speed.

The figure was structured like a blackened chariot with a shield and guard in the front. Its wheels ground against the iron beams, creating small sparks on occasion. The whole sight was terrifyingly mesmerising, for a being of such power had never been displayed to me before. It was hard to recognize my pursuer's impression of the iron beast, for they seemed to only continue the march. In a sense, it was poetic to see the two march on the same path, but I was between the two with notions of blocking.

I wasn't entirely defenceless, for the moon always watched over me, but the anticipation of impact still lingered as both closed in. This dream served as a direct lesson into becoming Father Drexel, and from what I had gathered so far, was that my mentor has been more than gracious to me when it came to saving my life. I needed to find a way to defend myself, without endlessly calling upon my mentor, for the moon was my guide and not my weapon. I needed to find my spark, whether it was the cannon fuse or the wheels along iron. Whatever it may be, it needed to be quick; something told me that this dream might be a rude awakening.

As the iron beast crept forward with longer strides, the water began to rumble with its automaton power. I felt my body shake against the iron footpath, beginning to question the safety of lingering on it. The thought of the iron footpath not belonging to me became more convincing with each rumble of the iron beast, blinding me sharply with its hypnotic glow. It grew closer, dangerously closer, so close that the rings from the cannon fought with the puffing smoke from the top of the iron beast! It took one more enticingly loud scream of octaves for me to move with a purpose out of the iron footpath!

In the mere moments I had left to spare, I watched as the iron beast collided with the air that occupied me just seconds ago. Its road shook me to my core, as it continued the speeding charge against the cannon! I was somewhat thankful to know it was stuck to the iron footpath, for the limitations of such a beast seemed relieving, yet cruel. However, seeing it from the side revealed how long its figure truly was! It seemed to never end, or at least in this realm.

To tell the truth, I was excited to see the collision, for the battle of the iron beast and the pursuing cannon seemed thrilling. As the iron beast was beginning to cross the line of the sign, the cannon seemed to take another shot. Oddly enough, it wasn't at the giant, but rather…. **the sign?..**

The sign fell onto the footpath with great intensity, blocking the way for the giant to continue! There was no way the iron giant would be able to stop in time; I feared its chase met its match with the cannon!

In a horrible notion of screeches, cries, and echoes, I watched as the mere sign managed to throw the iron giant off of its path, and fell to its side in a terrifying crash! Like an undeserved stack of dominoes, each of the giant's bodies fell as well, causing broken minds and shattered hearts throughout. The sound of each dying whistle pierced my ears, to the point that I had no choice but to cover them. I was speechless in the utter defeat of the iron giant; a being of such power against all odds! The echoes of its death never ceased, for the continuous cycle of its demise served as a taunt against both me and the giant.

It was hard to truly understand why the moon chose to show the fate of such a beast against my pursuer, for what could it all mean? I had not a single thought of what I just witnessed, all except the chills formed from watching the collision. I didn't want to listen to the dying cries of the future any longer, and called for the moon to take me home. Without fault, my mentor listened and everything began to fade. Starting with the sounds, the echoes dimmed with the darkness fading as well, as my consciousness returned. I beckon thee, one must always **strive to grow stronger.**

A Call from Heaven

I slowly awoke in my bed, feeling as if I had never gone unconscious, yet I knew that I had dreamed such a collision. The faint sounds of the roars on all parties seemed to linger in my mind, regardless of how much I yearned to forget the painful noises. That dream felt like the battles from Hell that the Man from Room #47 endured, but instead, an iron beast took the blows for me. I had to grow stronger, for no one should endure that pain among their soul like he once did. The motivation to continue coerced my body to sit up in bed, slowly letting my eyes adjust to the sunlight, for this was the first time in a long while that I was not beaten for sleeping past the break of dawn.

I still didn't quite know how to feel about my new, alarming dreamscape. I assumed that Father Drexel would see visions, but never something like that! If only I could ask him what everything meant, or even have some sort of hint to make it all sensible. Between my pursuer and the iron beast, I felt more alarmed by the white-cloaked figure, for they displayed that they could take on the utmost force, rather than just drugging me with fear. I was still more fearful of the tattered demon, but if the white-cloaked figure grew in any more power, I would feel utterly hopeless.

My pursuer never seemed to be aware of my existence, and was only after the iron beast's. I was afraid of the white-cloaked figure seeking revenge on me for my intrusion, but alas, it would be nothing new of Hell's creatures. A part of me didn't believe in my pursuer being a creature from Hell, for they looked pure in comparison to the bloodcurdling spawn of the void. Nevertheless, the deceitful aura that radiated off of their cloak was apparent enough to disagree. Maybe my world had collided with Father Drexel's, and had I accidentally sent a spawn of Hell to destroy my future with the iron beast, all while disguised with a mask of purity.

Deciding to stop lingering in thought for now, I looked around my room, and to my surprise, I saw a whole murder of crows scattered about! Many were perched on the bed, while others sat on the tops of the desk and along the wardrobe. They didn't bother me necessarily, but I questioned how they got in, considering my window was sealed shut. The minute they noticed my conscious state, they all flew out of the room through the window! I couldn't believe what my eyes beheld, for they seemed to phase through the glass!

No matter what entered and left my shut window, it was certainly better to wake up to the visiting murder than spawns of Hell. On the bright side, the peculiarity sparked me to get up a little faster. Getting out of bed and deciding to remake the sheets, I noticed that I was still somewhat drenched. My feet slightly slipped on the flooring, as my damp rags of clothing made me grow cold from the exposure to fresh air. One thing for certain was my need to change clothes.

I pulled the rags that I was forced to wear for days without end over my head, and gently tossed them to the corner of my room, for I had no real intention of ever putting them back on. They were stained with vermin and belonged to a man I no longer was, and I had no intention of revisiting either. Having no clothes on was an odd sensation; I wasn't used to it, from the lack of hygiene within Hell. A faint breeze brushed against my back, making me shiver from the cold water slowly drying. With drops falling off my hair and onto my back,

I anticipated the droplets to seep into my wounds, but I never felt that initial sting of pain.

Examining the rest of my body, it appeared that I had not a single wound upon my flesh! It seemed as if I had been miraculously healed by my mentor; a complete break from the Man from Room #47! Feeling elated, I thanked the moon once more and began to go through the wardrobe to find new clothing in celebration. I did not feel exhausted or any burn, for any noticeable trait of the Man from Room #47 no longer existed, except for my hair. I have grown accustomed to my long hair, and don't believe cutting it short would be of use at the moment.

I took the coat out and placed it on the bed, while checking for clothes to go underneath. I found basic dress clothes, consisting of button-up shirts and black trousers. Putting everything on, including undergarments, I finally felt like I was beginning to truly feel the role of the father of the Cathedral of Healing. On the top shelf of the wardrobe, laid a black hat with a large brim; it seemingly called me to wear it. Everything felt warm, secure, and dry through wool fabrics that grasped at my calves and a hat with a shadow-casting top.

The last thing I had yet to put on was the father's mask. The crow-shaped oddity slightly made me feel unnerved, but I convinced myself to wear it for three reasons; I needed to hide the face that was not truly Father Drexel, I needed to protect myself from the words of the letter, I needed to honour both the crows for their guidance, and also the father's previous choice. Taking off my hat to put on the mask, I noticed the large amount of herbs hidden away within the beak of the mask. I found it odd in the choice itself, but I chalked it up to a practice of his faith, or maybe it was in relevance to his power. The mask felt tight of black leather against my face, but secure in the same sense.

With the final conversion to Father Drexel, I felt as if I was ready to teach. The Man from Room #47 had almost fully left, and oh how wondrous it felt. I knew that it wouldn't be long until I was free from my past and could finally move on. Walking over to the desk, I looked to see if there was anything new to the eye that could be used as a muse. It was a different world inside of the mask, for it fogged easily if I didn't control my breathing, but it was manageable, nevertheless. The pages of most interest were handwritten notes on a small built-in shelf. Written in the father's handwriting were ideas for a sermon. Many were crossed out, but one was circled many times with much emphasis; it was fire.

Why did Father Drexel want to teach about fire? Many reasons danced about in my head, for the oddity of fire was an interesting, yet peculiar choice. Was it the danger of the flames' tongues, or perhaps something far deeper than I had initially anticipated? The questions of his teachings rang about through the room, as I debated how to approach the topic later. Wanting a better understanding of his head, I decided to adventure further into the cathedral, making sure to see the beauty of it all in the daylight.

Becoming the father of the Cathedral of Daylight was a very important title to bestow. Many people believed in this man, and now it was my job to continue the belief. I made a promise to both my mentor and the crows that I wouldn't come short, and that I would teach of fire. I would become the man to answer the finishing remarks of, "I am," and no longer see the Man from Room #47 as a person. Maybe once I master the teachings of fire, my dreamscape would become more clear? Perhaps I was to teach fire to the iron beast, and maybe my pursuer as well. I beckon thee, one must always **learn from fire.**

Midnight Sermons

Looking around the room for a muse, I saw the door that I wasn't acquainted with just yet. I took the sign of fire to explore its contents, and opened the door. The room was without a window, causing my eyes to rapidly adjust to the increasing darkness within. I was beginning to grow tired of the absences of light, and further used it as a will to find fire within me. Looking around with what I could, the room seemed to be quite small in size, mainly being a place of storage.

There were closets of robes and old instruments, with spare chairs stacked alongside one another. Nothing seemed too interesting, to say the least, but I did think of the small room as, if the moon was willing, a meditation chamber. I debated the concept of whether I should reside my feelings to the inside of the closet, or maybe within a chair. Deciding to get closer to my mentor by shutting off every sense, I swiftly climbed inside the closet and shut the door. The air was musty with a hint of forgotten nostalgia, like a comforting smell that was no longer cherished.

Inside the closet, I talked to my mentor softly, and sought guidance about what to do in regards to my dream. I spoke with the moon for many hours, it seemed; just my deepest thoughts and questions. My mentor seemed to answer every single question, with a silent voice explaining the importance of learning and teaching. I was told to never judge with only my eyes, and it made me ponder as to what brought up such advice. Was it the iron beast's persona of terror, or the white-cloaked figure's demeanour?

I was never answered with which being it was; I could only hope it would be answered through time. While never fully answering the reason behind the dream, the unsolved question turned into a new lesson for my sermon. The moon was the utmost helpful, but never precisely told me how I could obtain the fire. I learned how to engage with the audience, pull speeches to a close, and rally members, but never once was I told how to obtain fire.

Stepping out of the closet, I reconciled everything I had discerned, and felt ready to begin teaching in the name of Father Drexel, I am. My only question now was when would my teaching begin. The moon had no reply, so I took it upon myself to figure it out alone. I went back into my room and looked at the desk for the dates of letters, and maybe a calendar. After going back through time, using each little piece of paper, my conclusion held that they met on every Dimanche.

Ever since my endurance of Hell, I had lost the complete concept of time. I didn't know which day was which, or even the date of today; I'd be completely lost if it weren't for the years on the letters. Then again, all of it might be too old to matter, and I might be teaching dust on a seat, but the moon had sent me here, so I best complete my mentor's mission. I planned to await people's arrival within the Cathedral of Dimanche every day until the name of such aligns with the practice. I felt as if a fool could just as easily make this plan as I could, but it worked, nevertheless.

I waited for elongated hours, it had seemed, for the brightened day slowly drifted to grow darker. I predominantly resided in the main room of the cathedral, rehearsing key points I had planned to talk about, slowly watching the light dim from the stained glass windows up from above. I noticed that I never did tire from hunger necessarily; I always felt to my fullest. It was a strange feeling to go from constant starvation to feeling like a man of pure strength, for it all seemed different, thanks to the moon. The only hunger I felt was a sensational desire to learn from my mentor.

Soon, the day was a solemn ghost once more, with my mentor taking the crown unto the night. The light had ceased altogether, following the conductor's hands down. I was still left in silence within the Cathedral of Waiting, for I didn't want to leave without knowing which day it was. The thought of returning to the dreamscape of Father Drexel was not in my thoughts, for I planned to wait the remainder of the night; it felt like my mentor wouldn't allow me to sleep. I was like an owl, with sharp senses that extended into the night, as I flew from tree to tree in hopes of finding another pair of eyes.

I began to pace back and forth between each elongated seat, wiping and cleaning up in the process. It became harder to see each bunny, for the moonlight crept away from the cathedral quite fast. In the end, I mindlessly brushed my palms along each row, making sure to make every spot feel welcoming. As I finished the last row of wooden seating, I approached the front of the cathedral once more, towards the fairly sized wooden structure at the centre. It was the perfect height for me to lean on, like a desk for standing, or just for aching cages.

I stood behind the man-made table, facing the seats before me, and simply noticed how perfect the moon's gaze showed each spot to possibly sit in; a different angle of viewing was all it took to see it in perfect clarity. Looking at the small, lean table, I could see that the inside of the bottom was hollowed out with small shelves and a place for one's feet. I felt around for anything tucked away in the shelves, but found nothing except for more bunnies of dust. On the top of the desk, however, laid a large book with a crimson spine. Opening up the book to the page marked with a ribbon, were millions of tiny words on pages thinner than tangled hair.

I could not tell if my inability to read the words derived from my casted shadow, or from the words belonging to another language, but every word on the page could have been a dead fly. The only other reason I could think of was the mask. The lenses fogged with each breath I took, but the moon cleared them for me in the next. In these moments, I began to wonder how the father was able to teach in such a mask, for it seemed impossible to sound coherent! I knew I would find my true voice, whether it be from the crows, moon, or fire itself.

Any voice I had was completely lost, when I heard the front doors of the Cathedral of New Comings rattling. My steady breathing that I worked so hard to achieve was immediately ruined by my nerves taking over, causing my lenses to fog entirely. I couldn't see who was at the door; was it a student, the white-cloaked figure, or perhaps a wicked monster from Hell? Trying my best to calm down my breathing, I listened for the door to open. While my lenses began to finally defog, I could hear the sound of footsteps approaching the front.

When I was finally allowed sight, I saw a fairly dressed woman, with black hair to her shoulders, and a matching dress that covered almost all of her frosted skin. Without a word to her voice, she sat down in the first row.

That **grey scale**.... Was she?..

I was ashamed that my first thoughts were accusations against my new student for being the white-cloaked figure, but the noir and blanc colours resembled too much of my unnerving pursuer. Like the moon had said, I couldn't judge with only my eyes. She was more than the colours of black and white, for she was now a student under my wing.

I debated a million ways to approach a greeting, for I wasn't necessarily in practice of socialisation. She was quite charming, and brought a notion of interest within her; I felt little notes of intimidation, but it was certainly better than a drugging feeling of fear or regret. There was not a single thought within my mind telling me that she meant harm to **the great big moon in the sky**, and it was blissful to think such. To finally have a change in one's consistent dismay is a relief like no other, and I thanked my mentor countless times for peace finally meeting flesh.

As doubt infiltrated the herbs in my mask, I felt the utmost sense of dread. Anyone who came here before would instantly know that I was not Father Drexel! I reassured myself that it would all work out according to my mentor's plan, for Father Drexel was just now recovering, yes? It would be only natural for a man to recover vocally as well. The woman didn't seem to mind the lack of introductions and exchanged greetings, for she seemed to be in another world altogether within her mind.

Despite being under the moonlight, I could recognize the gaze of being elsewhere, no matter my mentor's smile. Her gaze wasn't in any particular direction, but it still felt like it was directed behind my mask, like she knew I wasn't Father Drexel. If anyone suspected I was not truly the father, then it was best that they left altogether, for they were not here to learn, but rather to deny the moonlight. I didn't want them to leave, but if that's where their hearts were, then their person needed to follow it outside.

Feeling less paranoid, more people seemingly began to sprout within the darkening rows. I found the time of night to have a lesson rather odd, but perhaps it was more unifying to sacrifice sleep within the name of learning. Every face's body that sat down amongst a row felt the same void of emotions and attendance as the woman in the front; nothing there, yet everything towards me. Nevertheless, they all seemed pleased to have their father back.

Every row seemed to have a few or more people within the seats, with each body seeming to have the same build and look. Every piece of flesh was whiter than Sibérie, and every strand of hair had a complete colour of void, with a matching suit or dress. I felt like this was a small lesson within itself to not judge people for what they look like. It could very well be my nerves, and the lack of human interaction catching and pulling my hair, but all of the similarities between one another made me want to believe that they were family. There was also the chance of the town's demographic consisting of such attributes, but it felt more welcoming to think of an entire family coming to learn.

However, the black and white family seemed to have attended many services in the past, for they all wore the wise minds of an excellent pupil. They knew more things about this world than me, and it was all the more intimidating. Once the last family member came inside, shut the colossally-sized crimson doors, and sat down in a row of seats, I took it as a sign to begin my teachings.

How should I even initiate the beginning? I had no concept of time other than it was the night of Dimanche. Should I bid a good night, or even a fellow hello? Settling with an answer that satisfied every worry of my own, I cleared my throat and spoke with forced confidence.

"It is well with the moon that I am here under its night, for I can continue services of thy cathedral," was all I managed to say without my words succumbing to my nerves. My voice seemed disembodied with my person, like it was on the outside of the mask, for it earned a faint, but noticeable, "*It is pure*," from the back of the Cathedral of Nerves.

It is pure; what an interesting choice of praise. Every time I spoke a line that they seemingly enjoyed, they exclaimed it once more. My mentor previously mentioned the goal of hearing their praise, was this their verbal form of such? I began to speak of my arrival by the moon, and every time I referenced my mentor's mission of guidance, gazes seemed to return to the cathedral, instead of drifting dreamscapes. All of the rows' focus was finally on my words, all except for the woman in the front. I wanted her to join us, for all I needed was just a little more time.

"I have foreseen the teeth of Hell, and I speak that none under my mentor's follow hath such flames under thee. Guidance from thy mentor bringeth fortune and deliverance. To dance against thee is to bring misfortune and dismay. I beckon thyself to make the choice of following towards and not against thy mentor. The reward of obedience is beyond compare, for I have witnessed the gifts of which thou bestows.

One may wonder what rewards from thy mentor make journeys alongside thee worth each struggle, but I say unto you, gifts contain the flames of promise. Each crimson flicker delivers a promise of protection and assurance. My journey alongside my mentor hath bringeth the role of Father Drexel. Can one truly deny a spark's blessing? Blessed be the souls under thy mentor's crow and flames."

The cathedral's walls seem to shake with ferocious intensity. In no case was it a malicious notion, but rather one of unison. I had finally grasped the consciousness of every man and woman that was willing to listen, and led them to believe in Father Drexel once more. The feeling was impeccable, for I felt myself growing closer to what **the great big moon in the sky** was leading me to find. My gift of protection and promise hid within the flames of each ignited heart inside the Cathedral of Praise, and it would not be long until the sparks of truth revealed themselves.

Every time they praised me with purity, I couldn't help but feel a sense of excitement. I loved being praised for simply talking of my past with **the great big moon in the sky**, and I felt my subconscious wanting more. Everyone seemed to love me, all except the woman in the front. She was still somewhat distant inside her mindscape, and never once spoke of the words, "It is pure." She seemed different from the rest of the family.

I just wanted her to listen to me, hear her voice call out to both me and my mentor, and finally have the satisfaction of truthfully having everyone's gaze locked with mine. After it seemingly felt like she heard my mental pleas and begs, her gaze locked on me, and radiated sensations of focus. I called out to her, as her face lit up with mixed emotions of recognition and curiosity. "Hath thou accepted thy new mentor? Art thou a spark of thy light?"

Her eyes glistened in the moonlight, reflecting her azure orbs and dilated pupils. While fond of my eagerness to teach, she seemed to match the tone at last in a soft voice, "I needeth thy fire to bring my spark to a flame, for **it is pure.**"

She needed my fire? Did she mean it through my words, or through a physical conflagration? I was honoured to finally be called pure, but the thought of her needing my fire overrode the sensation of bliss from the words of purity. I began to second-guess myself; did Father Drexel teach with literal fire, or did this woman see something I did not? I hoped that she only meant it in a sense of speech, but only time would tell. My nerves were coming onto me once more, for the thought of failing to kindle her flame caused me to be worrisome. I only derived my flame from the hearts and souls of others; it was not something I could easily bestow. I just needed more time.

I called her to step forth unto the front, and she did as such, with a flicker beginning to form. The eyes of the family were all entirely on us now, as the woman's gaze seemed more focused from the heat of her flickering light. She knelt before where I stood, and looked up at me. "Father, I humbly ask of thee to bestow your flame unto my spark."

I found it such an oddity that she persisted of my own flame, and not the moon's to help her own, but maybe that was what I was called to explain. "My flames of thee were lit upon my mentor, as which thou should follow as well."

Her gaze lost all focus for a moment or two, and it was somewhat disheartening to watch. I felt like I had denied her the right to escape Hell! If anything, I only wanted to guide her to the exit, but I couldn't do it with just a flame of my own. Suddenly, like the moon had rose in full within her mind, she stood up sharply and asked me, "Show thy flames for thy family to gaze upon, for a flame shown is another kindled, yea?"

The woman, who formerly asked for my flame, now asked to demonstrate under my mentor? She believed that by showing my own flame, it would kindle her own. It was apparent that my words of fire were not enough to create a spark; was I to form a physical light? I debated how to approach the concept of physical flames and tie it into the teachings, for I knew not where a candle or a spill laid. Suddenly, an ominous, yet faithful idea occurred to me; **what if I was the candle and spill?**

I knew that my mentor was offering notions of power through fire, but the concept of literal fire harnessed by my flesh seemed outlandish! Fire upon flesh was a former punishment for the Man from Room #47, but now was it the strength of Father Drexel? This strength defied Hell, and it would embody my purpose to guide others to the light.

I looked at the woman before me through the eyes of the mask, and then closed them gently. There was complete silence in the Cathedral of Echoes, as I lifted my head towards the moon. I followed with my hands, lifting the palms to face upwards together. They reached the same level as my chin, before they rested in the air, beginning to call out alongside me. I cried out to my mentor and exclaimed, "I beckon thee to grant my hands the spill of life, and use them to cast a flame unto thy hearts within thy Cathedral of Flames!"

My voice rang out into the cathedral, like a bell signalling the beginning of noon, and it was followed by a surrounding, rumbling vibration. I never once turned my palms or gaze away from the moon, but I knew that the faces of the family were in a state of intrigued shock. The longer I kept my gaze up above, the more I began to feel my palms heat up with a sensation of warmth. It didn't sting like Hell's teeth against the Man from Room #47, but rather a righteous notion of deliverance for Father Drexel. The sensation grew louder, with flickers of light emitting from my fingertips, slowly forming small flames along each nail and print.

I could hear the cheers and praise that came from the crowd, and a small, admiring sigh that came from the woman up front. I knew I had succeeded in conjuring flames within myself, but now I needed to gather them to make one, unified light. I put my fingertips together on each hand, and slowly formed fists, choking out the flame temporarily. When I opened my palms once more, the light was brighter than ever as one solid flame! Everyone cheered louder, matching the vibrance of the flames.

The flames lit up seemingly the entire cathedral with a warm, friendly hue. It felt cold to the touch of my palms, but I knew it would burn anyone else who touched it. My faith and role as The Father was what protected me from such flames, and the bewildering gazes among others confirmed the idea as such. I turned to the crowd once more, and held out my hands ablaze.

"What thou may see here is a manifestation of faith, hath thee such belief will result in the fiery passion of thy mentor! One may see that when thy mentor was called upon without strife, I was granted thy blessing of fire at my fingertips. When forming together, and persevering through a flameless pause, out will materialise a higher power than before. I say unto thee to unite together and grow a flame brighter than before!"

Many exclaimed colourful praises while others simply shouted another "It is pure," but the woman in front of me smiled greatly and simply cheered,

"Blessed art thou! Thy flames are pure! How **pure** thou art! Purity is among thee!"

I was ecstatic in hearing her voice praise me, for it sounded like the stars' songs of night. I couldn't help but feel a smile form across my face, and it caused me to shout, "To be blessed is to be faithful; it is in thou to conjure the same!"

The woman cheered and smiled purely, before returning to her seat. I waved around my hands ablaze, further embodying the notion, and then clasped my hands together. It formed a brighter flame, once the two conjoined in harmony. It never felt like playing with the fire, but rather cherishing the gift with combining each possibility to make new ones; it was all to help further teach the importance of faith. Never once did I want to release the flames out of my hands, for I wanted to simply hold the fire, as I demonstrated its purpose.

As my teachings survived alongside the flames, they seemed to grow with my passion and emotion. Whenever I grew louder, seemingly so did the flames. Whenever the family praised the cathedral's blessings with their "It is pure," the fire grew brighter. I felt so alive from it all, and with each praise I received, it only drove me to receive more. In almost a completely blanc hue, it lit the entire cathedral of flames inside; I began to understand why Father Drexel hosted teachings at night. It looked like the sun had crawled up already where any wall touched the fire's light!

I continued to teach until the room was too bright to see others, and the heat of the flame became unbearable. When the Cathedral of Flames had finally become one, solid ember, it was undeniable that the sun had breached the night. I ended the lesson with one final moral, and then clenched my fists to extinguish the fire. After the cathedral returned to the hue of day, the rows of family stood and left. Not a single soul stayed behind, with the black and white woman leaving last.

As she stood up to leave, she turned to me faintly with a quiet voice, "Thou art sensational, Father. Thy flames were holy in all eyes, for it was truly pure." I couldn't help but smile faintly at her words, for she had such a way of speaking to me. Being so close to her in the daylight of the doorway allowed me to see how bleu her eyes were. They never seemed to be directly upon me, for they were always through me or just to my mask. In the moments of studied silence following our small talk, she spoke three words that have forever reigned within my mindscape.

"Art thou family?"

I wanted to say yes with all of my heart, but something from the great big moon in the sky told me not to. I questioned the feeling at first, for I wanted to belong to this family, but I knew better than to disregard the moon's voice. Although I looked at her with more than my eyes, I failed to see where joining the family would not be in favour. It was soul crushing to look into those azure eyes and deny them of family, but with the utmost feeling of remorse, I spoke the words, "I am not a family member of black and white, but only under the moon's feet am I family unto my mentor. If thou art is under thy mentor as well, then so we are family."

There was a deafening silence, almost as to which a cannonfire should break free from. Her pupils immediately constricted from the sounds of my words hitting the ground, and looked directly behind my mask at the Man from Room #47. When I tried to look at her, I couldn't bring myself to look into her eyes. I was ashamed of failing to please her, and I felt as if I was impure. After a painful moment of silence, she gave no response, and simply walked away. Closing the doors behind her, she turned to face me once more. Her pupils seemed to have returned to their usual mydriasis, along with a faint smile.

"I hope to see you soon, Father, and I hope to see your flame grow."

With her final words spoken, she seemingly returned to her distant world as she left. I felt so guilty for denying her family, but it was better to deny the woman's than the moon's. Nevertheless, we could still be family if she accepted the great big moon in the sky as her mentor. Whether she accepted her new mentor or not was her own thought to have, for I had already materialised my fire.

The cathedral was completely empty now, and not a single sound was present. The busy, chaotic streets outside hummed in the distance, but never infiltrated the walls that I called home. I missed hearing this place be so lively, for I knew the next time it would be as youthful would be the next Dimanche. I missed the sounds of the roaring audience, and I missed hearing of my purity and flames. However, what I missed the most was the woman; I just needed more time with her.

Her praises meant the most to me, for they were always seemingly the most difficult to earn. She made me feel important, yet always made me feel guilty. I wanted her to see the full glory of the moon, but she never seemed to fully understand. I needed to see her again, I had to! I wanted to see her again, see her face look at mine, I..

They would come next Dimanche.

Trying to clear my head, I returned to my chambers, and into the closet. I spent some time thanking **the great big moon in the sky** for the successful lesson, and the gift of fire. I made no direct plans for the next lesson, and decided to let the moon guide me until the next night of Dimanche. I would continue to learn the ways of fire, and maybe project the flames unto other beings for combat. I didn't rush the offence, for the moon would let me learn only when it was needed.

I, now Father Drexel, finally found peace within my being, and promised to my mentor that I would spread peace to others, and help them follow the crows. I was no longer the man from Room #47, but I would never forget what he had taught me. Letting the moon be my guide, I would follow both my mentor and the murder to any time or place. I beckon thee, one must always **allow thy flames to burn brighter.**

A New World

I was with the moon inside of the closet for another length of time, as the day seemed to grow stronger in hours. We talked of channelling the flames within my palms, and further lessons to learn and teach. I was prophesied of a true change within my world, and that I should prepare by any means necessary. I thought about the meaning behind it all, for the chance of Father Drexel leaving the Cathedral of Flames was becoming a possibility. It was hard to comprehend the reasons, for I had just become the father of this place, but alas, I fulfilled my purpose. If it was in the moon's plans that I would be moved, then so it may be.

I debated how to prepare and ready myself, for the grand change wasn't specific. I didn't hypothesise that anything would change within the cathedral, but rather something outside. This place was the shield, my flames were the rapier, and my person was the armour. I thought of going outside of the cathedral and exploring the world that the moon watches over, but the concept of leaving the cathedral struck feelings of doubt combined with wonder. I left the closet and went into my chambers, looking outside of the window for a sign to explore.

The vision of day allowed no moon to surface; my mentor sent crows to watch among me. Gazing through the glass, I looked at the neighbouring streets and distant woodlines. Each building looked the same but different, with little camaraderies scattered about, and people dancing uncontrollably. The cobblestone streets looked pale, but the houses along the hills were pleasing to look at. The exposed timber with houses covered in greenery made me feel comforted, for it was much more appealing to the eye than the pitiful oak trees outside of the window from Room #47.

Before I could look at the dancers, the squawk of the crows dug me out of my focus. I looked at the three crows before me, and watched them plead for me to join them.

Once they flew off in the direction of the cathedral's front entrance, I took it as a sign to follow them. As I made my way through the Cathedral of Flames, my mind began to wander into the depths of doubt. What if I would be recognized as the man from Room #47, or what if the demon with black hair and bloodied rags from Hell ripped off my mask? It made me trip in step, for the fear of returning to Hell was stronger than I had initially recognized. To push past fear and continue the march was a difficult but necessary step; I continued to walk towards the door, even if I was at the point of discomfort.

Trying to think of the positives of adventuring outside, there was a chance that I might see the woman from the black and white family. I always felt so conflicted when I thought of her. I missed her, yet I wasn't ready to see her again. She made me feel happy, yet horrible when I made her eyes go against her pupils. However, the one thing to constantly eat at my soul was the fact that I wanted to see her face again, for I missed looking into her azure eyes. I wished for the crows to peck every feeling I had for her out of my person, for she was beginning to distract my flames from their full fire. I needed to focus on the white-cloaked pursuer and the iron beast, yet the woman made it so much more difficult. I felt like I could help her, oh how I wanted to help her! I couldn't wait for the next Dimanche; I needed to see her now!

I calmed myself, before I swung the cathedral door too harshly. While resting my hands on the crimson, wooden door, I took a moment of breath, before pushing it open. It creaked slowly, allowing my eyes to sharply adjust to the blinding sun. Even in a mask, the fogged lenses were still no protector against the rays of light. While letting my eyes reconcile with the intense shine of day, I began to notice that my eyes did not align just quite with my surroundings. The only thing that matched with my previous observation outside of my chamber's window was the crows' friendly stature.

It was impossible to let my lenses defog, for my breathing was absurd from the shock and disarray I felt. I no longer could trust my eyes, so in turn, I closed them tightly and listened to neighbouring sounds. The familiar sounds of birds chirping along with the squawks of the murder made me feel somewhat at ease, but a foreign sound of a hungry power hummed along the street. There were automaton beeps followed by inaudible voices that didn't embody a singular person, and music with instruments of a certain feeling of breath. All of the sounds came and went past me, everything but the familiar sounds of nature's trees and its fellow inhabitants, it seemed.

Dogs could be heard across the street from me, as I slowly began to calm my breathing. The lenses of the mask hesitantly unveiled my new world, and it was certainly nothing I could have ever expected. My cobblestone streets were replaced with smooth, greyed roads with a hint of death in the air, and the neighbouring buildings had grown in maturity and height. The architecture of everything had changed; some buildings even had a scarf of red silk and badges! There were symbols on each badge, but they meant nothing to me; they looked like a spinning cross.

The sky seemed a gloomy grey, with the clouds taking full charge. Each cloud had puffs locking arms with one another. Beyond each falsely decorated building were more clones of the same stature, for the woodline of my home was gone. Signs read of a language I couldn't understand, and oncoming voices spoke harsh, guttural sounds. No one seemed to notice me either, or at least give away the idea of collectively ignoring me.

Nothing looked real, for even the people of the new world seemed to exist only in dreams. Many people had azure eyes, with light-coloured hair following; ones with darker hair seemed to follow behind the brighter ones. However, never once was there a person with that black hair and frosted white skin. The clothing was completely foreign to me, consisting of different coloured dress shirts and suspenders. It wasn't that I didn't know what the items of clothing were, but rather what they seemed to represent. It felt like I was an intruder into this new domain, and that some might have the audacity to exterminate me.

There was a specific group of people that I deemed the most unwelcoming, due to their thunderous appearance and gloating attitudes. They were far away from me and the crows, but I could still see the clothing that they were wearing. They all matched with black, slick, knee-high boots, and similar jackets and pants. Some were decorated with pieces of unknown shinies, but the one thing they all wore was a red armband on their left arms. They walked together in unison, creating a thunderous march down the road; it was truly like the rumble of the iron beast…

Where was I?…

I questioned why the moon had brought me here; who was I to spread the message of the Flaming Night to? It was painstakingly obvious that I was no man of thunder here, and I grew increasingly worried that it would cause conflict in the future. Nevertheless, I trusted that I would be able to protect myself, if the boot marchers would cause any dismay towards my person, or the Cathedral of Flames. I will admit that I felt as if I was growing sick, or even an urge to dance until death; a part of me wanted to return to my chamber, and maybe even preach to that wonderful family of black and white once more. However, every thought I had of taking a step back was always interrupted by the squawk of the murder.

I didn't feel forced into this new world necessarily, for I still could push past the words of the crows, but their words would only make more sense if I followed them. Taking a deep breath in and slowly letting it out, I made my body relax a bit, before I shut the cathedral's crimson doors behind me. A part of me accepted that this would be the last time I would touch these oldened doors, but I knew better than most that faith must reside in the person, and not the place. I looked up at the crows, and nodded my head slowly. With an elegant flap of their wings, they began to fly into town, serving as my faithful guide.

I still felt the tiniest moments of tension, as I progressed into the town. All of the unfamiliar people and places were tempting to look at, but like the man from Room #47's waltz with the moon, I couldn't break away from the crows. I knew that if I dared to look away from the murder, I would lose sight of my guide entirely, and be stranded in the new world. The terrain that my feet walked upon was a peculiar feeling, for it may be the new boots I had acquired as Father Drexel, dancing with the feet of an uncivilised man from Room #47. The ground itself was smooth, and let me glide along the road with ease; it felt like I was flying among the murder!

I couldn't tell if I passed any strangers, but I knew I had passed the furthest building I initially saw. The gloomy building of fine stone left my peripherals, and became completely foreign, as if I wasn't already a stranger. It was a complete mystery to me as to where the murder would take me, but I had to overcome my nerves with faith in the moon's judgement. Passing the last building seemed to open up my field of vision completely, and changed the terrain I walked upon. It felt like loose rock; something I was more accustomed to.

The crows found their way to a nearby tree, and resided there to judge my ability to follow. With twisting heads and swift twitches, the murder declared me to be one of their own. Finally feeling at ease to break away from their gazes, I looked to see where they had led me in this new world. My eyes widened like a madman's, as I felt my body bend over uncontrollably. I couldn't believe what I was brought to see! On top of the loose rocks' hill was the iron path once more! Like an infant's first word, it marked the beginning of understanding the new world.

At last, I was beginning to comprehend the reason for the new world, and my purpose within it. I wasn't to see the woman, but rather the iron footpath. Now that I understood my gift of flames from the moon, I was sent here to escape all distractions. Whether or not I would teach, avenge, or fight the autonomous creature was unbeknownst to me, but I felt ready for any of the possibilities. Fighting the iron beast was definitely the most unnerving option, but I was ready if the moon and crows allowed. I looked up at the crows once more, after identifying that it was the same iron footpath from my dreamscape, wanting further guidance. While they never answered my question, they welcomed me to follow the iron footpath once more. I beckon thee, one must always **be ready for change.**

A Walk With Thy Mentor

The murder did nothing but squawk at me, and flapped their wings towards the iron footpath. As much as I wanted to deny the truth, it was inevitable that I would travel down it, like I had as a man with no flames. Slowly stepping into the middle of the two parallel beams, I began walking into the undefined future. On both sides of me were scattered trees surrounded by open fields, with notions of a hidden evil behind the juane scenery. Even nature seemed to have underlying tones of deceit, for what laid ahead of me was a land of disorienting oddities. The sky was still as grey as stone, and the vegetation seemed to only swell from the gloom as well.

I let go of all focus on the woman from the black and white family, and devoted my mind and soul to **the great big moon in the sky**. It would be of no use to dream of her now, for I was here to travel down the iron footpath. The crows followed me, but still stayed a distance behind; I was the guide now, and I had to lead the crows without hesitation. We walked along the iron footpath until the new world finally granted something foreign. In the distance, it looked like a fairly sized mountain, dark in rock with a…giant **hole** in the bottom?

I couldn't believe how nature would form such an extravagant being, but as I grew closer to the mountain, it became evident that nature didn't make the hole at all. With the smooth finishes and engravings around the entrance, it was no secret that it was a man-made tunnel.

Looking into the insides of the mountain was unnerving, yet somehow promising. I was bewildered with the technology here, and could only presume I was in the future, for the tunnel inside of the mountain only proved it. Alas, I was in a time where man moved nature, and saw it as nothing but a hindrance to their path. The inside echoed as much as my dreamscape did, ever so slightly ringing my ears. Nevertheless, this tunnel was made for the iron beast, and the roars and whistles it produced could override any scream or cry.

I was paranoid of going inside of the tunnel, for the thought of the iron beast meeting me inside definitely invoked fear within me. The tunnel was large, but the iron beast with another man inside would definitely test the integrity of the tunnel's walls. There was no other way to continue the path without going through it, but the tunnel, at least, looked fairly short. I looked behind me to see what the crows might think, but to my surprise, the crows followed me into the tunnel, and even landed on my shoulders and arms! With the murder perched upon my shoulders, we were completely covered in darkness while entering the tunnel's mouth in full.

I walked calmly through the tunnel, trying my best not to spook the crows, for if they flew away in a hurried cry, I would follow them, no matter the outcome. Thankfully, they stayed upon my shoulders for quite some time; I managed to even make it halfway through the tunnel. The air was bleak and muggy, for puddles of water slept tucked away in the cracks of the tunnel's corners. However, near the middle of the tunnel was a hole in the wall. It did not lead anywhere, but it was deep enough to hide from the iron beast. I was thankful to know that someone along the way feared the iron beast enough to save themselves, but also many others to come after them.

I wanted to press my hand on the back of the hole in the wall to better gauge the depth, but I was worried of the crows growing afraid of the tight space. Instead of using my sense of touch to simply find the depth, I decided to simply use sight. Raising my arm for my hand to meet the inside of the hole, I put my fingers together and released them to form a small flame. It wasn't much of a light, but it was enough to see that it would store my person in case the iron beast were to appear. More so, the crows were not bothered by the fire at all, for it was my gift from them to begin with.

Deciding to keep the flame in my left hand as I walked, I used it as a guide out of the tunnel, now crossing the halfway mark. The crows were well-behaved, and never made a sound; they knew it would hurt my eardrums as much as theirs. It wasn't until I kept my flame at hand consistently while travelling down the tunnel that they decided to squawk and flap their wings, seemingly warning me of my fire. I didn't quite understand their reasoning for such a commotion, but I silenced the fire, nevertheless. They silenced themselves after the extinguishment, but they seemed off.

Leaving the tunnel, they all seemed to be paranoid, constantly looking around and twitching about for answers. I will admit that their constant questioning was making me grow jittery, for it felt like my own faith was uncertain. I looked all around me and saw nothing, so I could not even begin to understand why they were going mad! There were no autonomous creatures, no tunnels left, and no boot marchers in sight, so why did the crows seemingly go into a frightful panic when I had released my flame past the hole in the wall? A thought occurred to me once I gave a moment to rest in thought.

Did the fire signal my presence? I thought surely not, for no one was around me when I conjured my fire, but what if I couldn't see them? I turned around to look at the tunnel once more, and all my eyes could see was darkness. I looked at the crows, wanting an answer for their sporadic behaviour, but they had already left me, and were now perched on top of the tunnel. I was bewildered by their action to abandon my shoulders, but I knew it meant that things were becoming increasingly grave.

I looked around my surroundings for another check of safety, but all I continued to see was the darkness of the tunnel. The tunnel was dark, as dark as my dreamscape, and as dark as the void of the iron beast's previous scene. The dark tunnel would have swallowed my fire whole with the shadows of the man-made cave; maybe that was the reason the crows had abandoned me in such a rush? No, it was not, for the reason was much darker than that, darker than the lightless tunnel itself. I paused for a moment, and felt myself grow drastically frail;

where was the end of the tunnel?

I began to panic like a madman, as my heightened senses allowed me to finally hear the rumble of the iron beast; It was coming straight at me! It bore no light in the day-time, unlike how its eyes pierced into me during the night of my dreams, for the light it possessed was hidden to further sneak upon me. It hissed and whistled its harmonic shrills, as it came burling towards my fearful state of person. I had to do something, think quickly, just move! Allowing myself to think for a moment or two, I remembered in a sporadic thought that it could not move off of the iron footpath, for it was like its own cage.

In control of my own body of Father Drexel once more, I threw myself to the right of the iron footpath, past the beam, and jumped into the loose rocks trailing into the grass. I landed in the same position as I had when the man from Room #47 escaped from Hell, but unlike him, I managed to break free without a singular cut on my body. A roar of the chasing iron beast rolled past me in a maddened blitz, forcing my mindscape to realise how close I was to not making it out of the parallel beams at all! As I stood up slowly with a shaken core, I turned to the iron footpath once again to see what remained of the iron beast. To my horror, it had completely disappeared; the only thing left in sight, other than my observing murder, was a gravely man on the other side of the iron footpath. I beckon thee, one must always **be ready to make the choice to save one's own life!**

The Iron Beast

I was left speechless when staring at the man on the other side of the parallel beams; every time I looked at my crows for an answer, they would return the same, stiff-postured stare. Returning to stare at this man once more, I began to feel very grave myself. This man was like no other; he wasn't like one of the men in the black and white family, a stranger from the new world, a boot marcher, or even a demon from Hell. This man sent new notions of a being never quite discovered before, and I was the first to do so. Similarly, yet opposite to me in another sense, I felt like this man had more to himself than what met the eyes.

His stance seemed at ease, but stiff enough to be harrowing. He was tall, but not quite as lanky as me; he could go into the mountain's hole in the wall without bending over. The only thing that would hinder his ability to fit into doorways was his top hat. Its skin was made of a black silk, with a red ribbon around it. The tophat wasn't too tall, but enough to express a higher class.

However, his hat did not match the rest of the outfit, for he wore a tan coat with length around his legs, with many pockets and buttons trailing down in parallel lines. It matched the clothing from this new world, but not at all in the same sense. The quality of his clothes never matched the other, like he found them one at a time in various places. His shoes matched the ones of the unnerving boot marchers, and I almost believed him to be one, but unlike the boot marchers, this man had longer hair. It was nowhere in comparison to my hair, for mine was a tangled, chestnut mess.

His hair came down to just below his chin, and curled like a madman with black, greasy locks. However, from his ruined tophat to his new coat, the most unnerving notion about him was his mask. It was utterly faceless, bearing porcelain skin with no mouth, nose, or eyebrows; it was a completely flat mask, with nothing but eye sockets. Even then, the holes were a black stain, for I saw nothing of his eyes. The simple, disturbing mask just continued to stare at me, almost like he was provoking me to make the first move, or perhaps he was just studying me like I was studying him. I knew that the next move was crucial, and that it might be best to make it myself.

The only conceivable question to ask this ominous man was,

"Qui es-tu?"

I tried my best to make my voice sound clear through my own mask, but I was still worried it would be a futile attempt to connect. I was proven to be correct, as he remained deathly silent. I doubted his ability to hear me the first time, so I let my voice grow louder,

"Qui es-tu?"

He seemed to mumble something that time, but most of it was unintelligible, slurred words, all except for a faint, *"Wie schön."*

The man was German? I had a growing suspicion that I was in the country of Allemagne herself, but it didn't do me any favour, for it meant I lacked a way of communication. I knew it wouldn't be that easy to simply travel the world with the crows without a hindrance, for we were now separated along the iron footpath by our mother tongues. He spoke German, and I spoke French. In hopes of him knowing any sort of English, I tried my best to speak once more,

"Who art thou?"

"I'm the **railroad man**,"

Those were the first words that he spoke to me. His voice had a low rasp to it, but his accent was undeniably harsh. I had not the slightest idea as what to do or say, for it was apparent that he was from a time ahead of me. I didn't want to ask about what he meant, so I simply hoped that time in the new world would answer everything for me. My English was rough in itself, for even my period's standards.

It was hard to focus on the concept of who he was, for his hollowed eyes made me lose focus every other bleeding moment. I assumed that the word of the railroad was the same as the iron footpath, which now begged the question of his relation to the iron beast. Before I could ask him about such, he asked me a question of his own. Despite his masked mouth, he asked with a harsh accent,

"Vhat ist your name?"

His tone was cold and calculated, and it hummed that he knew something I did not, like there was a card up his ripped sleeve. I debated whether or not I should reveal my name as Father Drexel, or simply my position, like the ominous railroad man did. His ever so slightly different choice of words made me choose to state my position as well, for him knowing my name might evoke a power of sorts.

"I am the Father of the Cathedral of Flames," I replied.

I wanted to know what he would ask or say next, so I had more time to pull words of a language I barely remembered; it was the work of the crows that I managed to converse this much already. I was trying to ask him of his relation to the iron beast, when he completely interrupted me with his own question once more.

"You don't look like you're from here. Are you lost, or are you just eager to meet the Third Reich? Nazis aren't too polite towards frogs, ya know."

I didn't quite know what to say, for my words were taken, just like my orientation was. His way of speaking was almost impossible to decipher, from his words of the future to his accent. I tried my best to answer him, but also allow my question of his relation to the iron beast to crawl inside. Although the questions of who "Nazis" were and what the "Third Reich" was, I decided that the iron beast was more important.

"I don't know of what thou speaketh, but I was sent here by thy deliverance of the iron beast."

"...You mean like a Bahn?.. Iron Beast, das ist rich, haha! The word you are looking for ist a train, Froggy."

I couldn't understand him well at all, and was beginning to grow ever so slightly frustrated. I knew it couldn't be helped, but I wish the crows could speak my mind in the utmost fluent German, and have his replies translated into French in an instant. I didn't know how to respond for a multitude of reasons. Between the overwhelming accent and new words, I just chose to stay silent. If an iron beast was called a train in the future, and a bahn in this new world of Allemagne, what was a froggy?

I didn't push the new words' meanings any further than the railroad man would take it. Having no choice but to let the conversation flow down a fogged river, it was impossible to see the end. Unlike the bliss of my previous fog, I finally felt the urgency of knowing the end.

"Well, what is thy relation to the *train?*" I asked.

He responded with a ghastly tone,"I *take trips to the promised land, und I do vith the locomotives as I please...* Think of them like your flames..."

...He knew of my flame? He seemed to read the confusion on my face through my mask, and continued without skipping a beat.

"Yes, I know about you; your flames are quite vibrant. You valked through my tunnel vith your little crows, but it looked like all you can do ist let your little light shine. Can you do anything else?"

"I don't know, for I only listen to the crows above who guide me in power."

He looked to my crows, and spoke "Vell, vhat are your crows telling you now?"

"That I was destined to meet thee."

"Vell, if those bird brains are right, then you must be in for one hell of a time. I have been on a small excursion myself to find the hellspawn of a creature that tried to stop me in my tracks. I don't think that you are the one to be them, aye?"

"No! Why would I?"

"Of course a frog like you vouldn't. Vhat are you here for then? It's not every day a flame-throwing plague doctor valtzes into Deutschland"

"I believe in thee being my aid in this world, if it is in the moon's favour."

"Vell if it is, then it starts with you learning to use that gift of yours to its full potential; be a flame thrower und not a damn candle. Your gift from your little crows vas fire, but it takes the strength of man to use its full potential. The crows are not violent creatures, so they'll never teach you true offence, but man is a creature of violence, and I can definitely show you vhat it is like to be violent."

I questioned why he didn't kill me then and there. I was clearly blocking his path, and wondered why I had yet to be run over by a *train*. We were connected through power, and likely through the great big moon in the sky, but he was so much more than me. Perhaps I was sent here to be an understudy, and help him find the pursuer that likely bonded us? It would only work if I proved my worth to him, but I feared the end of the river's fog.

"I am not a man of violence, and I refuse to join such!"

"I never said you had to be violent, just more assertive than your delicate light that could be snuffed by a little boo. Ve have both seen Hell, ja? I only escaped through being **assertive**. You can only run zo much, und Hell doesn't have to take breaks to catch its breath; it eats and consumes like fire. I see something in you, und it's too valuable to be burned alive."

I slowly began to understand the mysterious railroad man, but I still felt like I was not to use my flames for such wrath. Time would only tell for whom the flames would burn, but I was willing to learn how to conjure a fire from man. The crows sent me here to meet the railroad man, and now it was time to learn from him, and possibly teach him of **the great big moon in the sky** later.

His mannerisms never spoke of him being with me, but always a step ahead in action, time, and thought. The railroad man didn't bother to ever take the time to see with his eyes at all, and seemed to only judge with his sense of feeling. He didn't see me as an equal, but only as a frog. Nevertheless, it was better than being seen as a fresh kill. From the look of the railroad man, he was ready to teach me the way of man, and if I didn't learn from him, his future wouldn't be affected ever-so in the slightest. I beckon thee, one must always **be ready to hear from the wise.**

The Lesson of Faith and Life

"Step onto the track,"

Said the railroad man, so hauntingly simple. His arrogant nature had left his body, and returned to the former phantom across the rails once more. With my back facing the tunnel, I watched the railroad man join me on the iron footpath. He stood across from me, with the familiar feeling of a grave notion behind his mask. Once we were both settled between the parallel beams, his lesson had begun.

With a small hint of a smile in his voice, he spoke. "I control trains, the progression of man, vhat do you do?"

"I conjure fire, the gift of the great big moon in the sky."

"You may, but you don't control it. To have control over your fire inside is to have a balance in your character."

I looked at the supposedly balanced railroad man with a sense of disbelief. If anything, he seemed more disoriented and unbalanced than anyone else. He wandered with no purpose, and only had a goal of murder. I felt the slightest amount of ridicule from his comment towards me, but I decided to keep in tune with what he had to say, for maybe what he deemed to be a balancing act could help me. With him not explaining any further, I simply asked, "How doth thou find balance in thy character?"

"You have to find vhat traits make your fire better. It might take more strength, it might take more flexibility," said the railroad man, as he looked through me, and into the tunnel. I could see his character work alongside his power in that sense, but I still did not understand how his mind coincided with the iron beast. It made no sense for a man like him to bestow such a powerful machine, but alas, this was a new world filled with the future. Wanting to know the truth behind his abilities, I asked him,

"How doth thou summon trains?"

The railroad man laughed a little bit, before he deeply exhaled into his mask. Watching his body change before my eyes, his stiff body relaxed in an unnerving way, almost like he stole the bones from a healthier man in the process. Then, with no focus in his hidden eyes, he began to defy the stars themselves with a move like no other. He leaned backwards with one leg following, and his arms losing all notion of life. They gracefully dangled, as his head met the ground, and one leg met the sky.

It was a slow, uncharacteristic move on his part, but it was perfectly smooth and balanced. I finally understood what he had meant by a balance within character. A cluster of stars could be of any brightness, shape, size, and hue, but all it took was an apparent line within them to make a constellation. That line between each star was what balanced the cluster, and gave them the title of a characterised constellation. This railroad man, who I had previously deemed to be a black hole of the night, was actually the constellation of Cancer.

As he continued to let his feet stand above his head, I began to hear the familiar, horrifying sounds of the harmonic whistles. That was how he summoned the iron beast; he called them with a calculated balance with his boots reaching for Heaven, and his head reaching for Hell. In this balance, he called for nothing but his own character. When the chilling multiphonics surrounding me seemed to cease, so did the railroad man's balancing act. He continued to lean back upwards in a controlled manner, without a grunt or stifled sigh.

I will admit the fear I felt was greater than the man from Room #47's journey out of Hell, for a man with no faith that had such balance was morbidly terrifying to me. I turned away from him and to my crows once more, silently begging for an answer to all of this, but I was interrupted by the railroad man loudly clicking the weighted heel of his boot against the tracks, followed by him raising his finger to where his lips hid, and made a silent, but seemingly echoing "shhhhh." I felt sick to my stomach, and wanted to snap him out of this creepy trance. I tried turning to my crows again, demanding them to stop the railroad man, but he marched louder this time, and followed his thunder with another "shhhh." His march progressed in power and speed, to the point of the tracks rumbling themselves!

My legs vibrated against a combination of the roaring iron footpath, and my ever so trembling legs. If his goal was to intimidate me to conjure my own flames, then he was certainly succeeding. I felt my back growing increasingly hot, with the flicker of flames in my peripheral vision and hands. I had to prepare myself quickly, for I sensed that the lesson of balancing my flames was already in session, and I just gave headway to the railroad man's point by uncontrollably materialising the fire!

I couldn't control the flames any more with this amount of fear, and it almost felt like they were beginning to burn me! Every time I wanted to call upon the crows, the railroad man creepily shushed me and continued his march, eventually turning into a full sprint towards me! He didn't care about the fire, for his character matched the bleeding persistence of the iron beast at last! The crows never left their spot on top of the tunnel, but they still continued to stay silent over my seek of aid. I didn't feel betrayed, but I couldn't understand anything that was happening; from the iron beast to the solemn crows, I knew this had to be done.

I felt my flames burning my back, and I yelped from the pain. Was it actually my flames, no, it was a train! Its eye of light was adding fuel to my fire, but it was not a fuel I could control! I jumped off of the track once more, barely escaping in time once more. Looking up to see if the railroad man did as well, I saw that he was still on the track!

Just when I thought he was going to get hit, he lazily stepped off of the track, whistling to himself. I knew he was in control of the train, but it was still completely soul-shattering to see the railroad man treat such a beast with little to no regard for his own life, if he even still possessed one. "That's what true control looks like, Froggy. *Get a hold of your throttle!*" He exclaimed, both taunting and trying to get me to explode with uncontrollable fire once more. I jumped back up from the ground, and conjured flames within me to materialise in my hands, still somewhat questioning the meaning behind being called Froggy.

I charged towards him, watching my flames grow in luminosity with the increase of adrenaline and speed. He seemed thrilled to finally see me lose composure, as if this were some childish game! He immediately took a swing towards the beak of my mask, but it almost seemed like he was deliberately being slow with his movements. I ducked under his blow, and went for his now-opened chest. Picturing him as a doctor from Hell was all I needed to successfully land a hit into his- arm.

He blocked my jab to his chest with one of his arms, and I could see him reach for my wrist. He was increasing his speed of combat, and the aid of fire was not slowing him down. He acted like his presence was enough to extinguish the flames out of fear, and if I was honest, it would be true. I had to keep my head with my body, and continue the balance of power. I kept myself angry, and tried to remind myself of the railroad man's insults to both me and my crows.

The railroad man dodged a kick from me by jumping backwards. The distance between us allowed him to be open enough to do a backflip into the air, letting his boots and head meet Heaven and Hell once more. I screamed in frustration, not knowing where the train might come from. Hearing the returning screeches, they were seemingly coming from somewhere other than the tracks! I wanted to look to see where the hollowed voices laid, but it was impossible to not be hit by the railroad man, unless I was studying his every breath!

The rumble of the iron beast returned, as I could see its blackened body in my peripherals. I quickly jumped out of the way, and so followed the railroad man. He seemed to laugh at my fear, and followed his joy with a contradicting kick to my mask. He managed to hit the beak, but not without his boot being scorched. In the quick, fearful moment, I had managed to travel the flames within my body to my head, and into the mask's beak!

He grunted a bit, before dragging his boot into the dry grass, as a way to save what remained of his boot. In the same movement, he switched legs and did another backflip. My small victory seemingly now turned into a loss, for it felt impossible to get that man to stop challenging both Heaven and Hell! The harmonics returned with another cry, and thus the train materialised. The railroad man was ruthless, for he charged at me, and kept me in the train's direct line of destruction!

He pushed me to the ground with a grunt and a half, forcing me to either get hit or burn him alive! Screaming out of both anger and fear, I turned my whole body ablaze, further ruining the railroad man's clothes and skin. He masked his pain with another cackle, as he rolled off of my body, creating the same pattern of defying Heaven and Hell. It was infuriating to think that the only way to stop this man from conjuring the trains was to light him on fire without my body doing it for me! Scrambling to get out of the way while dodging endless blows proved to be more difficult than anything else I have ever done, for the threat of the railroad man was more dangerous than the ragged demon from Hell!

Before the railroad man was able to get back on his feet, I grabbed him by his charred boots. He lashed out in an angry yell, kicking and calling me obscured words I didn't even understand. He started to grow uncontrollable within his own mind, and I began to feel as if I was making some sort of a lead. Thanking the crows for the temporary victory, it became a standoff of strength. He began to force himself into a sort of handstand, but I would not let his legs progress his head.

He began to shake and convulse, almost as if he was trying to shake me or his boots off. I kept a firm grip around his ankles, increasing the fire that went within them. I didn't plan on stopping until he cried out for mercy, or I felt as if the crows wanted me to stop. He twisted around to where he faced me, and pulled me in with his knees bending.

I fell forward from the sudden jolt and up he went, while kicking me in the progress. I felt pain in my stomach form, as I made sure to scorch his legs again, before I gave up to protect myself. I jumped back up, remembering to keep close, and followed through with more combat. He seemed to slow his offence; he was growing tired and became more defensive. He stayed in place, but stood guard quite well. Every time I tried to push him into backing up or to another direction, he stood guard and landed a blow, only onto my mask.

I was beginning to feel better than he was, and it fueled another spark within my step. My kicks seemed to flourish with fire, and even lingered in the air. Each was a direct hit to him or his clothes, and each burned piece of fabric was a win to me. I had not yet gained full control to project a flame onto something else, but I knew it was only right around the corner. The railroad man seemed to sense this too, for he began to dodge my kicks and laugh maniacally.

"Time's up, frog man!" He cackled wildly, before charging straight towards me. He didn't care about the fire in the air, he only cared about grabbing my neck with the grip of a dead man. I was completely taken back in shock, losing all wind at once. I began kicking my legs and fighting all I could, burning my handprints into his forearms, but he would never let go. He dragged us onto the tracks, and kept me hostage against the beams, whilst kicking his foot backwards and over both of our heads.

The railroad man was deranged, and practically foaming at the mouth in anticipation of the iron beast! "That train is going to **kill you**, if you don't set that damn locomotive **on fire!**" He screamed at me, forcing his grip around my neck to somehow clench tighter. My vision was losing itself, but even through a fogged mask and dying vision, I could still see the horrendous beam of the iron beast's eye. I tried the best that I could to lift my arm towards the train, and conjured something within me that knew it was life or death. I put my faith within a hidden part of me that was breaking in, and exploded a flame that took everything within me, including my sight. I beckon thee, one must always **have faith in life, and life in faith!**

Inside the Great Locomotive

There was a great flash of light, an intense heat, and an awaiting sense of burning metals piercing my flesh. However, when I opened my eyes, I seemed to be inside the train. There was no longer a dead man's grip around my throat, and to be quite honest, I didn't care where he ended up at the moment. Both my vision and my mask seemed to clear, as the noises of the train grew with clarity. I could hear the turning of wheels running over the beams, the wind that beat the passing windows, and the distant sound of muffled music.

The air was musty, and the carpet I now laid upon smelled of faded smoke and alcohol. I slowly brought myself to my own feet, and found a sigh of relief in me to see that I had little to no injuries. Sitting down in a nearby seat, I noticed the crimson fabric-lined seats, like the ones in the Cathedral of Flames, matched the lighter carpet and trimming. The rest of the fixtures were of cherry wood and blanc marble. Setting my hat and mask down on the table, I leaned my head back in the satisfaction of emitting a flame.

I didn't feel balanced, for my head was still spinning and chasing persistent questions for my crows, and the new orientation of a face without a mask. Nevertheless, I still felt victorious, and looked around the room for the lost railroad man. All I saw were the same fixtures of marble and wood with doors on either side of the back walls. The one closest to me looked to lead to the main head of the iron beast, and the other seemed to only lead to another door. I was the only one in this room, and the thought of that was just enough unnerving to make me no longer be relaxed.

I didn't think it was safe to leave the train while it was still running, so a part of me needed the railroad man. Thinking about him caused the exact same double feelings, for I hated him, yet I appreciated him. Even now, I didn't necessarily want to see him at all, but I knew it was futile. His train was comforting enough; maybe he wouldn't be such a disgrace.

The soft music coming from nowhere in particular was rather soothing, for it almost lulled me into a dreamscape. It hummed of brass and foreign languages, but it was still a whimsical little tune. Breathing in fresh air without a mask, I almost smiled from the sensation. I didn't mind if the railroad man saw me without it or not, for he would have no knowledge of the man from Room #47, or Father Drexel. I closed my eyes briefly, slowly nodding off, but the fade into sleep was cut short, when I was awakened by the sound of the far door opening and closing.

A gust of cold wind followed behind the railroad man, as he approached me with a faint limp in his step. It didn't seem like he had any injuries, but the way he walked seemed to be in effect from his charred clothing. He looked like a walking corpse, when he sat down in the other seat across from me. The railroad man sighed a bit, leaned his head back against the seat, and then looked at me with a notion of nothingness behind his mask. His breathing paused a bit, as he seemed to finally notice that the so-called "frog" actually had a face.

"So that's vhat you look like, eh?" he said bluntly without skipping a beat. "I suppose," was all I wanted to reply with. I didn't feel like feeding his ego anymore, yet he always found a way to trick me into doing just the opposite. He pulled out a metal bottle in the shape of a rounded square, and unscrewed the tiny lid on the top. While drinking seemingly all of it in a moment or two, he asked me in between drinks, "So did you see the flame projection?"

"I could not see for the lack of sight my eyes gaveth, but I felt the power."

"You can thank me later, or not at all. For now, ve celebrate. I had to put my flask up, thanks to your little flames. Imagine me, lit up like dynamite, all because of some ol' booze, haha!"

He chuckled a bit before returning to drink his apparent alcohol, leaving me with a slight distaste in my mouth. He had his mask slightly lifted off of his face, just enough to drink away. I couldn't make out any exact features, but his mouth was definitely scarred from each corner. It could have been the shadows playing with my eyes, but it seemed that parts of the flesh on his cheekbones seemed to have rotted off at some point. It was unnerving to say the least, especially how he seemed to envy my own flesh more with each drink.

Wanting to distract him from his booze, and me from his corpse, I began to ask him more questions. "Thou never spoketh thy name," I said with a quieter tone, in hopes of making him put more focus into the conversation. He took a few moments to reply, but he finally spoke,

"I'm a lonely soldier, good man, I'm Mr Lonely."

Mr Lonely, what an odd thing to be called, yet such an understandable name. The life of a man escaping Hell was lonesome, for no one truly understood the horror we had to endure. The only ones to understand were my crows, and Mr Lonely's flask. Regardless of motives and beliefs, we knew that we could understand each other on a level no one else had before. It was just Mr Lonely and,

"My name is **Father Drexel.**"

His gaze seemed to finally come to look at me, instead of right through my skull, once I spoke of my name. "Drexel, that doesn't sound too French. Maybe it is, and I'm just a foreigner, hoho!" he oddly cheered, while raising his bottle once more. "Why are you so persistent about mocking me?" I asked with a small hint of annoyance in my voice. He laughed a bit, before finishing off his flask.

"Well, for starters, I hate frogs. However, now that we've exchanged names, I can hear you a bit better; I won't have to listen to that blasted French accent constantly."

He paused a bit, taking the time to screw the lid back on before he continued. "Once a man introduces himself, I've noticed that things just become clearer." I asked about why he only chose to exchange names now, when he clearly had the chance to before, but his only answer was a slurred, "I thought you *pushed brooms on the Delavare Lackavan,* hoho!" I wasn't surprised anymore, for he never failed to put himself higher than me. I thought that we were somewhat equal now, but it certainly had its advantages and disadvantages.

"If I'm French, then you're German, yes? I heard you mention that we were in Not See Germany?"

"Nazi Germany, yes. French people aren't liked too much here. As for me, it's hard to say; I've been here for quite some time, just rolling along the tracks. Sometimes I leave them to find a new pair of socks, sometimes I leave them to find a purpose. It used to be killing Nazis, but now it's a goal to find that damn person who shot me in my tracks."

I felt my face grow numb, and a small notion of sickness that crept up the back of my throat. I knew what he was referencing, but did I dare let him know? He might kill me for not helping him, or even just witnessing his downfall! I wish I could console my crows as to what I should do, but the train was long gone from the tunnel. I knew that he referenced such earlier, but I didn't know he was referencing the dream I was bestowed upon! Nevertheless, I had to decide by myself, and it felt gut-wrenching to do so.

"I think I dreamed of that as well. Was it someone in a white cloak with a cannon?"

"Yes, did you get humiliated as well, or did you just want to share dreams with me, jaja!"

I wanted to tell him what truly happened, but I didn't know if he'd even believe me. In the end, I decided to let him choose what he thought, and I'd go along with it. "Even if you were in my dream, I don't think I saw you. It might have been before you were even a flicker of light, which is still odd as to how you were even there. Normally, people with power are connected, but considering you probably didn't have a fire at that point, someone must have really liked you," he remarked with a smirk.

I thought of my crows, and then of my mentor. I thought that I was gifted that dream initially from earning the title of Father Drexel, but now it seemed as if I was destined to have that dream from the moon regardless if I was the man from Room #47, or the father of the Cathedral of Flames. On the other side, I thought of the woman from the black and white family, but I knew that I couldn't see her until I helped the railroad man. In moments like such, I felt motivated to learn the ways of fire in order to avail her. In the end, I just needed more time. Thinking about such made me question Mr Lonely's story, and who he was before his inevitable crash from Hell. He was never too specific with any part of his life, but I was determined to get some sort of information out of the mysterious railroad man. Looking straight at Mr Lonely, I asked him the question that plagued my mindscape.

"What's your story?"

"Why do you want to know?"

"Because you've revealed nothing about it. You at least know that I am a teacher, so why not reveal at least something?"

"What good would it do?" he lightly taunted. I knew where this was going, and as much as it made me angry, I would bite the bullet in order to better understand him. I fed into his ego, and told him how it might inspire me. He seemed satisfied with my answer, and ultimately obliged to tell me his story in full detail. With a final hidden smirk formed underneath his mask, he returned to a solemn nature to tell me his story of Hell.

He sat upright for the first time, and then rested his arms on the table in front of us. He spoke of his childhood, career, when he met Hell, how he escaped it, and how he carries on now. Supposedly, in the future, Amérique du Nord would grow powerful, and control forty-eight little countries. He couldn't recall which border he resided in, but he could describe the beauty of the green mountains for hours. He always described them as a luscious, lively scene, with much praise from the whole world.

It seemed to be the only thing he remembered about his home before Hell, but alas, it was one more thing than me. He compared the mountains in Allemagne to something similar back to his home, but never quite right. When talking about the events leading up to Hell, he mentioned something of his work. It was what sent him here, and ultimately to Hell itself. He talked of the demons that plagued him, and how pristine the uniforms that they wore were.

The way Mr Lonely spoke of his demons reminded me of the boot marchers I saw in town. When I asked him of such, he explained that those were in fact his demons. I was bewildered as to how they seemed human in flesh, yet monsters under skin, but I didn't want to press him on the matter; all of our demons were divergent.

"Hell was more than a burning pit of despair; I never could properly breathe. Every unintelligible question led me to less air. The further away I was from the air, the more I knew I would never see it again. Through time, I was a choked soul, in desperate need of relief. It was the lowest I ever was, and I have no thought of ever meeting such a fate ever again."

"How did you escape?"

"Same as you; I broke out. Unlike you, I managed to get hit by an oncoming train. Whether it was the grace of God, or his punishment for losing faith, I woke up not a minute later alive, but in critical condition. I could see my own flesh being held together by strings of muscle. Only when I managed to watch my leg mindlessly fall over my head was I rescued by my locomotive.

Slowly, I began to realise the correlation. I stayed inside the train for a long time, slowly healing day after day. My bones were mended, my ligaments seemingly in one form, but never without a scar to remind me of it all. Once I was able to function as an undead creature, I began to go out into the world. I didn't have a particular goal in mind, except to gather clothing.

I robbed many of their prestigious garments, and decorated them with my flesh, as a sign of revenge. It became my livelihood, and a magnificent way to strengthen myself. Whenever my clothes were stained or ruined, I went ahead and got a new pair. The only things I have yet to replace are my hat and mask. These are one of a kind, and I refuse to part with them just yet.

I'm not that deranged to try and replace my skin just yet, haha! Thanks to you, Father Drexel, I have to get new boots. Find yourself guilty to know that a demon's blood will be on your hands; you're not so holy after all, hoho!"

I took in his story slowly, thinking about his beliefs and motives, and the story in whole. The railroad man bore the clothes of his dead demons, and found merriment in retrieving them! He was never truly gifted anything, but truthfully fought for the right to even stand. His balance came from training, and the sickening duality of mind he had. It was somewhat admirable to see his work ethic, but disturbing to see the nonexistent limits he was willing to strive past. Now that he feels seemingly bested by the white-cloaked pursuer, he was ready to give it his all to slaughter them, and that also meant forcing me to do the same.

He was ready to leave the train and salvage more clothes, but I tried my best to keep him inside with more questions. "What do you know about the white-cloaked person with the cannon?" He grunted a bit, sitting back down. "They're this person that targets people like us. I don't know where they are, or even who, but people with powers like these are drawn to each other, like a moth to a flame. I don't know when, but one of these days, I will see their cloak in flesh."

With his final remark, he got up from the seat and slowly walked over to the nearest door. Every time I tried to start another conversation, he would answer with one word and then continue to the door. It took a probable ten mindless questions to get him to stop advancing the door.

"You just never stop, do you, frog!?" he yelled harshly.

"And you don't either!" I retorted back.

We went back and forth for a moment or two, but it ultimately ended with a door being slammed shut, and only one person left inside the locomotive. It was I who stayed behind, for I did not want to be associated with a murderer, demon or not. It was not my battle, and I certainly did not want to join it, or anything near the word death. Another thought that crossed my mind was that my crows were not outside, and that was enough of a sign not to part with the train and into the deathly adventures of Mr Lonely. I wasn't German, I wasn't a Nazi, and I had no business here anymore, for my sole purpose here was to find the railroad man and project fire. I needed to stay pure, for both my mentor, and the woman from the black and white family.

I didn't quite know what to do, except wait for the railroad man to come back with spilled blood. The sounds of the train were no longer comforting, for I was reminded of the horrible power it bestowed. The train seemed to increase in power and speed, making me feel light-headed. I wanted to look out the window for the first time, but was stopped by a black curtain. When I pulled it back, it revealed…..a black void?

Were Mr Lonely's trains in some sort of purgatory until he wanted to use them? I pondered on the thought, until it hit me that he hadn't summoned a train to murder anyone just yet. I was surprised by the fact that he hadn't jumped to the first pair he found, but I suppose that he was a man of quality, and wanted the best for himself. Suddenly, the void crashed into town! Hundreds of buildings and bullets went flying all around, before an inevitable thump in the front.

I ducked under the table quickly, readying myself for an ambush of uniformed demons, but alas, the only monster to board the train was Mr Lonely and a new pair of slick, black, knee-high boots. Before I had time to look out the window again, it was already black once more. I looked back at him with tired eyes and simply asked, "Who was it?."

He only responded with a faint, "A deserving one."

He stopped briefly to get out a glass and bottle from the cabinets above, and spoke with more rasp in his voice than usual. "Sorry it took so long, there was a guy in a white coat who kept nagging me about not having a pure heart. I ended up taking an extra second to enjoy the silence afterwards." I shuttered at his words, just imagining the white coat being so mindlessly stained, even after they talked of purity! Nevertheless, I was just somewhat relieved that he only robbed the 'deserved one.'

Assuming he meant his uniformed demons, and not the poor soul, I sighed while watching him leave to the next room over, carrying his drink and glass with him. I decided to follow him slowly, carrying my mask and hat with me. He led me to a small hallway with doors on both sides, humming a little tune to himself while doing so. I was rather confused by the oddity, but Mr Lonely told me to simply pick a room to sleep in for the night. Opening the door next to his choice, I stepped inside while giving thanks to him for the place to stay.

We had agreed to get up in the morning, and meet in the dining cabin. For now, I was to get some rest in this little room that consisted of an average-sized bed with white sheets and a red blanket. The rest of the room consisted of empty cabinets and shelves. Everything matched the same interior design of the dining cabin, and the overall welcoming feeling of the Cathedral of Flames. The only thing that did not match the same feeling was the tiny device on a nearby shelf.

Upon further inspection, it looked to be some sort of futuristic music box. When I cranked a knob on the front of its face, it turned to this piercing sound of distortion. Playing around with the other knobs and switches, I finally managed to make it play a coherent noise of German music. It was better than nothing, and it oddly made me feel relaxed. Something about it reminded me of my black and white family from the cathedral, but it grew to sadden me, once I realised that we were over 400 years apart. I hadn't thought about them in a while, and I began to feel distant mentally. I missed them more than usual, but I knew that I couldn't let it get to my head.

I just needed more time...

Deciding to turn off the music box, I got into the bed and exhaled slowly. I could see under the curtain from this angle, and could only imagine that **the great big moon in the sky** was out there somewhere. There was definitely a progression in speed and power, not by the train, but by the moon itself. I felt ready for the next time I would face peril, and I felt as if Mr Lonely was as well. I beckon thee, one must always **understand why character is built.**

81

The Frosted Stop

That night, I had the same dream of the camaraderie of cosmos calling me, before sending me to the void to see my pursuer. However, after the final waltz with the stars, the void changed drastically. The air was frigid and I had no warmth, due to me taking off my coat and mask to sleep. I was forced to use my flames to protect my shaking body, who was only clothed with the mere flesh I thought I had left behind from Room #47! Despite being in the flesh of his, I knew that I was him no longer.

The water along the void's floor was frozen over, and I could feel my feet wanting to stick to the ice. My pursuer effortlessly glided along, and followed every flicker of my flame. It felt like a pitiful game of cat and mouse, for the white-cloaked figure could skate amongst the ice, leaving me frozen. The painful dream reminded me of Hell, and it only made me think less kindly of my pursuer, and how they might truly be a demon.

I was growing dreadfully fearful, and wanted nothing more than to escape. The pursuer was growing increasingly deadly, and wanted nothing more than to have my fire. The dream only ended once I finally extinguished my flame from exhaustion; everything went black from the lack of light, and so did my unconsciousness. The white cloaked figure had no use for a flame not in use.

When I woke up, I realised that I had laid as a dead man until mourning. I didn't plan to tell Mr Lonely, for I feared his ridicule of not defeating the icy heart of the white cloaked figure. Waking up to the chilling air of the train cabin made me pull the covers over my body tightly, and made me regret taking off my coat before I went to sleep. Still tossing and turning, I decided it would be best if I went ahead and got up for the day. Slowly putting my coat on, I debated looking out my window.

It seemed brighter than usual, and it was ever so drawing me closer. Pulling back the curtain gently, I saw the void to be pure white, as white as a bright light in the sky. I was puzzled, and wanted an answer to the change of scenery; it hurt my eyes while looking at its face! I left my room in a bit of a rush, and out into the dining cabin. I carried my hat and mask with me, and sat them on a table once more. Taking my seat, I awaited Mr Lonely to join me, for I was the only one seemingly up.

I awaited his arrival for elongated hours, but he still never showed his mask. Not wanting to wait much longer, I took it upon myself to go to his room. Travelling to the next cabin over, I stood in front of his door. I could hear faint noises coming from the other side of the door, and it beckoned me to further listen. I was confused by the foreign music, for it no longer sounded of harsh, guttural words and sounds, but rather smoothly rolled, fast voices. All of it was still foreign to me, but I wondered if it was Mr Lonely's real mother tongue.

The music was immediately turned off, and was followed by a very much-needed sigh. I took it as a sign that he was now up, and quickly left back to the dining cabin. Swiftly sitting back down, I tried to calm my breathing, in hopes of appearing less suspicious. In a few minutes, Mr Lonely came into view with a slow, but purposeful attitude in his stature. He walked over to a nearby cabinet, and pulled out two mugs with frost around the edges.

I couldn't tell if it was the cold air of the room, or just the design, but it was surely a luxurious look. He went around the room without uttering a word to me, before pulling out a pot and pouring this brown liquid into both of our cups. It smelled rich, like bitter chocolate, but I was still weary of its full contents. After finally sitting down, Mr Lonely tipped his mask once more, and began to drink out of the mug. I waited a few seconds before following, just to see what the liquid would do to him.

Observing that it was safe to drink, I sipped a little before looking at the railroad man madly. "How do you drink this?! It's so bitter and sharp to the tongue!" I tried my best not to spit it out, but it felt nearly impossible! "It's coffee, frog. I figured you would've tried it before, but I guess I'm not as wise as I think, or maybe you're just uncultured," Mr Lonely remarked, as he poured himself another cup.

"Perhaps you like tea?" he seemed to ask with a sort of sarcasm in his voice. I never tried tea before, but I was sure it would be better than coffee! He hastily got up and retrieved another pot, before getting out a small box of little bags. "Pick which flavour you like, while I get you a little teacup," he said while sighing a bit, seemingly disappointed in my preference between the two. Smelling each bag, some smelled of fruits, while others of mints; the one I settled on was of a blueberry hibiscus.

When I was served my new drink, it tasted like the glorious moon's dew, compared to the unbearable rays of the sun that was coffee. Mr Lonely scoffed at me many times, but it ultimately made me laugh. It was the first time I had a drink since Hell, and it was my first time laughing as well, but this was the first time I had ever felt an earthly comfort. I thanked the railroad man many times for the drink, describing my times to him in Hell and how the tea reminded me of my cathedral. I began my story to him, and described to him my knowledge of the cathedral. When I spoke of the black and white family to him, that was the only time I seemed to grasp his attention.

"Black and white… What was it like to have such an audience?"

"It's hard to describe them as an audience, for I saw them as my own family. They supported me so much, calling me pure, and praising me to quite a degree. I felt unstoppable from it all, but now I feel empty from the lack of voice. There was one woman who was very vocal about her love for my flames, and often asked to have or see them. She even wanted me to join her family, but ultimately didn't; I wish I had more time with her. She was so pure, and seemed to have such a hunger for more."

"What was she hungry for? You? Hoho!"

"No, she was just eager to hear my sermon, and I was more than excited to help."

"Look at that! Father Drexel has feelings for someone other than his crows! Jajaja!"

"Stop that, it's not like that… She was a pure, curious woman who wanted to see me summon fire, even before I knew I could do such a thing."

"That sounds odd, don't you think?"

"No? The original Father Drexel preached of fire quite often. There was no way she could have meant it literally."

"Then how did she act once you materialised fire from your literal hands?"

"She was amazed, like I was myself! She had faith in me, she called me pure! She was happy for me! She was eager to learn how to do it herself!"

"Do it herself? And did she ever manage to do it?"

"No, her heart wasn't towards the moon. If I had just a little more time with her, I think I could have helped her."

"Have you seen her since?"

"No, when I went to go look for her, I ended up here. Now I'm talking to a railroad man."

"Well, unlike your woman, I'm actually listening."

I scoffed at his words, and couldn't help but feel a sense of disbelief. He wasn't happy that I met such a woman, but rather had a distaste for her! He thought of her as no different than the white cloaked figure!

His constant belittling made me feel angry, for I knew there was no way the two were connected. That woman never made me feel so fearful as our pursuer did now! Every time I told him something of how I thought of the woman in black, Mr Lonely kept repeating, "But does she actually?"

If the woman was the white cloaked figure, that meant she was related to the tattered demon! There was no way her purity was in relation to such a beast! "I'm sure she's pretty, but look at the facts. She only wanted your fire, and to see if you were willing to give it to her. You don't know anything about that woman, other than what you think is this aura of purity. If you want my opin-"

"No, I don't! She just needs guidance, and you're making her misguided curiosity look like evil! I just need more time with her-"

"Shut up, you lovesick frog. That schwarze und weiß woman wanted your flames, and was willing to hurt you for it. She chose to do it mentally, and I see it's still working. She didn't take them then, because they were pitifully small. Your flame has grown now, and I can guarantee she'll be back with her whole family to harvest it.

People with power are connected, and people with power can take another's if wanted. The only reason I haven't taken yours yet is because you make nice entertainment, frog or not. The white-cloaked pursuer was after my locomotives, and I refuse to let anyone live that could possibly think they'd be able to take them away. Whether it's your so-called "pure" woman or not, I will make sure that I personally burn them *in ol' 97's firebox*. I know more than you think, and I don't think that I'd be wrong, especially when talking about frauen. Besides, I'm sure we'll see your real demons soon; we never truly escape them until we kill them ourselves. They'll come to us, one way or another. If we see the black and white family again, rest assured that they are nothing but your bloodthirsty demons."

The concept of meeting the black and white family with a possible new view of faith was unnerving, but I knew it couldn't possibly be true. Why would a family go to such lengths, all in order for me to succumb to their demands? Why would the woman make me feel so happy, all just to supposedly strip me of all of my faith? I didn't want to think about it any longer, so I changed the direction of our conversation, as I poured myself another cup of the moon's dew.

"What languages does the music box in the rooms speak?"

"It picks up stations nearby, so it should be only German. Though, this morning, it sounded like it was speaking in Russian."

"Why is that?"

"Beats me. Maybe I've finally been caught, hoho!"

"Have you bothered to look outside? It's all white! Take this more seriously!"

He huffed at me, while opening up the curtain between us. His charismatic stature immediately faded into the void, as he gazed into the purely blanc world outside. He was utterly speechless and frozen like the snow outside, and only broke the frost when he turned to me. "Well *give me a handout, and revive me again!* Why do you always manage to make everything difficult? Between your tea, fire, and now your demons, you've done nothing but make life miserable. However, I will say that your misery has made it more challenging, and almost fun. Come on, frog, let's go see what you managed to make follow us."

He got up, adjusted his mask back over his face, and put on his tophat as the train stopped. I followed with one final sip of my moon's dew, and then decided to put my own mask and hat on. Before strapping the bird's beak back over my face, I exchanged the herbs inside of the mask with more bags of the blueberry hibiscus bags. With a fresh smell, I joined Mr Lonely at the door to the exit. As he opened up the door, we noticed different things about the new terrain.

I noticed my crows were back and perched on a twisted tree with hardly any green showing; they sat there silently, not causing a commotion, but rather a quiet greeting. Mr Lonely noticed the snow tracks of many pairs of boots heading up towards neighbouring trails and hills. In the distance, a village could be seen, but camouflaged by coldened white blankets. The freezing wind bit at my hands and any exposed piece of flesh, but I knew I had to progress alongside the railroad man. This new world had overtaken even the most powerful man I knew; the journey here would certainly mean being reunited with the black and white family, but only if they were related.

If **the great big moon in the sky** was willing, I would find the family, fight the demons from Hell, and follow my murder until the end. It was currently unknown as to why we were brought here, but judging from my mentor's visions, I'd say we were being invited by the white-cloaked pursuer, and my own personal Hell. I beckon thee, one must always **be able to accept the colours of the grey-scale.**

Finding Flames of Thee

The snow crunched beneath our feet quite loudly, whether it was us being as silent as a grave, or just the severity of the snow. I thought it was peculiar how Mr Lonely seemed to walk along the snow, for he always rolled his feet, and the rest of his upper body was completely still. He was a phantom gliding across the stage, but I was merely a young dancer, still not used to pointe shoes. It was difficult to walk in such snow, for it came up to our knees, biting my flesh underneath my trousers. I looked like a madman walking with my knees, rather than feet, but it was impossible to walk with my shoes in this weather!

I didn't want to use my fire just yet, for there could have been people watching who were just waiting to pounce. I felt visible enough as it was, using my crows as a guide, and wearing my outfit of an apparent priest from Francia. I never knew of what Father Drexel was, until Mr Lonely explained the emblems on my cloak. I felt guilty for teaching something in his name that he didn't entirely believe, but maybe his god and my moon were the same. It felt better thinking of that possibility, rather than simply disgracing his legacy.

The murder gently flew above us, and began to lead us into a woodline. I could feel the doubt growing with Mr Lonely, but I assured him that they could see more than us. He thought it was idiotic to follow into the woods, when a visible village could be seen ahead with foot tracks leading towards it. I had offered the idea of splitting up, but he insisted that we stuck together. In the end, it took the value of the crows foreseeing my demons to get Mr Lonely to follow.

Stepping into the treeline, I felt hidden from any lingering stares, and thought it was safe to use my fire. The air was much colder under the arms of the trees, but all the more questionable if my flames caught a limb. I decided to conjure my fire, and cast it onto my feet. Finally, I had joined Mr Lonely in the danse across the stage in a major key as well. I made sure not to take too big of a step, for the risk of burning everything around me like dominos was growing to be an increasing threat, as the trees seemed to grow in size and army.

Neither of us talked to each other; we were both distant within our own minds. I was focused on the crows, while Mr Lonely was focused on our surroundings. Eventually, the silence broke between us when I saw that the trees were thinning out at last, allowing me to finally see the crows in whole. When the last tree seemingly faded, the crows turned around and sat on the tallest limb. Mr Lonely pulled my attention to look before us both, and saw a new, snowy village.

This place felt darker than Francia, and even darker than Nazi Allemagne. Looking at the colourless buildings reminded me of the black and white family, and the snow looked to feel like the notion of chains never quite letting go. Not a soul was outside, and the air felt dead. The wind pushed it around like a body in a wheelbarrow, and pushed every house as well. This place felt abandoned, but the only thing keeping life here was the inability to escape.

We never walked onto the main road in the inside of the town, but stayed on the outskirts, examining each and every window. All of the signs were useless, for they were written in Russian with no English translation. Most of the insides of buildings looked to have people inside, but none matched the feeling that hung over this fairly sized town. No one had that noir hair, but the blanc skin seemed to be something everyone had. Perhaps it was a brand of the snow? I was fearful of any head of hair that dared to be noir; I hoped to the moon that the black and white family was not here!

As we ventured into more populated areas of the town, the snow seemed to lessen in strength. Thinking it was safe to walk without fire, I extinguished the flames that I had originally bestowed to my feet. I missed the warmth on my legs, but I had to persevere for the crows. I turned to Mr Lonely to see if he had a plan of any sort, and not to my surprise, he had already taken the lead. He immediately took us into the inside of town, not caring who saw us or how we perceived our own.

"I don't believe that my trains are the best bet to live in anymore with this place. There are no railroads anywhere here, and I doubt that these vodka drinkers wouldn't notice a random locomotive. We need a building that we both can hide in, until we finish everything here. Either you pick one and make peace with the people inside, or I pick and win a matryoshka doll set. Right now, I'm looking at that little house on the edge of the street. It looks fancy enough to suit me and you, don't you think? Hohohoho!"

I sighed, knowing it would be of no use to explain that a fancy house likely meant important people. I desperately looked around the place to find some sort of abandoned building, but, alas, all of the buildings had a candle lit in the windows. I wish my crows would have followed me into town, and helped pick out the right building, but I knew that the murder would not approve of what we were doing. I wish I knew an alternative option as well, but not a singular thought or solution came to my mindscape. Were we supposed to live in the woods, or were we supposed to find the cloaked pursuer before nightfall?

In the end, I settled on living inside the big family manor, but not without being hidden from the family itself. When I proposed this idea to Mr Lonely, he agreed to the "fun idea," but if either of us were caught, then he would become master of the house. The house itself was on a hill, and proved to be rather challenging to climb. The gate in the front of the building was easy to climb over, but not without it becoming a friendly competition of tricks. As expected, the somersault of Mr Lonely's easily beat the pull-up that spun over the gate of mine.

I was fearful of a train blowing our cover, but one never came. When I had looked at him with a questioning glance, he simply remarked, "Do you think I can't control where they go? Don't worry about it, froggy, haha!" I huffed at the insult, before walking behind the manor's privacy trees. The two of us made our way around the house, and decided it would be best to look around the back, before we decided to look inside the main building.

The snow continued to come down in thick flakes, but never without somewhat covering where he had previously stepped. It was getting harder to walk again, but I knew I couldn't conjure any flames. People of the same power always managed to sense another, and I didn't want to risk it, especially after the train departure. Someone was controlling more than we wanted, and I couldn't afford to give them any more cards. I returned as the unskilled ballerina through the manor's garden, as Mr Lonely walked through with ease.

The remnants of the garden were something I did not expect to feel as melancholy as it did, but I knew that the frost would be lifted someday. After passing through the frosted garden, we managed to see a small, but still a fairly large building out behind the main building. I was worried about someone being inside the building, but the candles were not lit within. The roof was impossible to tell of its colour, due to the blanc blankets, but its walls were of a worn brick. Even though the door we first saw was a faint, pretty green, and had easily seen its better days.

The condition of the building in whole made me somewhat mirthful to know that it was clearly rare when this family came here, but the off chance that this place was to store their objects of winter made me nervous. We walked around the whole building, before we realised that the only door to enter was right in front of a nearby window from the family manor. Mr Lonely had offered to keep guard while I found a way to open the door without making too much of a noticeable change to it, but I did not have the first clue as to how I should go about opening it. Mr Lonely was ready to break it down if I couldn't think of anything fast, but then I had the simple thought of, *"What if the door was already unlocked?"* Dumbfounded by the discovery of it being completely unlocked, we silently crept inside.

The air was stale with the smell of mould filling the air rather sharply, but it was better than the smell of copper and stained carpets. Frost was on the windows, with boxes and crates of childhood toys and family relics stacked along the walls. This place was home to the family's past, and we were intruders. The bottom floor held decorations for different seasons that were larger than most, with a creaking staircase that led to smaller boxes. The second floor also had a small area with a few blankets and scattered toys; a hideout for children in the summer.

Mr Lonely was the first to pick a spot, and began to look at the toys. One he held up in particular looked to be two dolls, one a boy and one a girl. They both had pure, white hair, but contrasting outfits, with one consisting of a red poncho, and the other a blue robe. I was surprised by the railroad man's behaviour, for I witnessed him put them up with a sort of ease into a nearby box. I didn't want to push him on the matter, but I enjoyed seeing him in such a nice way.

"The door into here doesn't have a lock. We need to barricade it for now until we depart. I don't want to take any chances." His new change of person shocked me, and made me no longer able to suppress the urge to ask. "I thought this was a game, no? What did those dolls do to you?"

He had a moment of silence, but slowly turned to me and spoke.

"I'm not quite sure, but I feel connected to them. Not to the children who played with them, but something about who the dolls might be. Maybe I had a pair like this of my own before Hell, or maybe they look like someone I know? It's hard to tell, but I know that the little dolls are pure, and can't fight against anything. We can, and the family inside can as well; I'd fight them for those dolls."

It was nice to see a code of honour of sorts with Mr Lonely, for I now knew that he wants to protect the pure, but what he labels pure and infected is a whole other matter. Perhaps he took what was pure off of others, whether clothes or dolls? I looked at the toys on my stack of blankets and pillows, and found them to be nothing but little decorated eggs. They weighed more than I expected, but still managed to stay small within my palm. I put them in the dollhouse as well, as Mr Lonely moved different boxes and assortments in front of the door.

When he came back up the groaning, wooden stairs, I decided it was time to make and discuss a plan to find answers as to why we were here. The black and white family and our cloaked pursuer were likely to be related, with our pursuer being the woman herself. It was easy to assume that they were connected, but we still had to find evidence, and more importantly, find the reason for their torment. My mentor has shown me many things leading to this place, and it has only made me believe that I would purge this world of Hell. The final step was how I would go about it. I beckon thee, one must always **have a plan ready.**

The Schoolhouse

"So how do those crows of yours talk to you?"

"They don't necessarily; they're more like a sign, instead of a voice. Why do you ask?"

"Because your little friends are outside."

I turned to the window, and as the railroad man said, the murder was there! They were a beauty to see such black lightly dusted with snow. I felt a notion of reassurance wash over me, and looked to see what they came for. They didn't seem to be fixated on anything in particular, or in a hurry to leave, so I simply assumed that they were here to listen in on our plan. I was content with letting the murder be our plan in whole, but under my flesh, I knew it couldn't be that simple.

"What do you think they're here for?" Mr Lonely asked me, leaning against a wall, facing the birds and me.

"Just to let us know that we're on the right path." I looked at the crows once more, furthering my questions as to what we should do next.

"How do you think we should go about finding our pursuer?"

"We've been using your crows a bit; I'm sure it wouldn't hurt to do it again."

I chuckled a bit at his response, for I didn't think that his ego would let him admit to following crows! When I teased him on the idea, replies of insults and defences were thrown at me as fast as a locomotive, but I knew it was all in somewhat of a light-hearted joke. The stir ended with the decision of heading out into town, and looking more into the people, rather than just the frosted windows. We would find if the black and white family resided here, and finally settle whether our pursuer was in relation to the woman's supposed loved ones. The only problem now was when to initiate the odyssey.

It was optimal on both sides for us to leave as soon as we could, but settled on a new way of exiting. "Maybe the crows want us to go out the window, instead of the door? There's a chance that there are eyes that way, and the window faces the back." My offer to follow the crows out the window proved to be the better option, but not without allowing a possible peril to form. Opening up the window, I forced it upwards, breaking the ice in between the cracks in the process.

The murder quickly flew away, and allowed me to step onto the slick leverage of the window's lip. The man from Room #47 dreamed of jumping out of his window to end his misery, but now I, Father Drexel, stood upon the ledge to ascend higher by dropping lower. The ground was a ways from here, but I hoped that the flesh of snow would aid my fall. I will admit that there was a slight ounce of fear within my knees, but the soothing thought of snow comforted me. Taking one last look at the murder above me, I jumped off of the ledge.

There was a minuscule moment of tranquillity, as I fell freely within the air. Although the time I spent in the air was less than a second's worth, the impact was impeccable. My mind searched every memory I had to relate the feeling of falling to a place before, but this was the first time I had ever freely fallen. To achieve a dream of another while still chasing one's own is a peculiar journey, but nevertheless, I was not a stranger to it at all. I tried to land with my feet first, but it ended up being an angled movement of my back taking weight. The snow comforted me rather snuggly, but not without its teeth biting into my exposed flesh.

The temperature difference was incredibly harsh, for I laid in the snow in utter shock, slowly looking around me in between shivers to see if anyone had seen my exposed flesh. Nothing seemed to be exposed; the woodline had a perfect blanket. Above my head, I could hear the railroad man telling me to move with a quiet, but annoyed tone of voice. Trying my best to scurry out of the way, I moved to the side, but still protected from view. Like an aerialist, he perfectly jumped out of the window, tucked his feet to his chest, and began to fall in flips.

He managed to land on his feet, right on the impression of where I formerly resided. Mr Lonely seemed to be unphased by the temperature difference, from his breathless stance and dormant posture. "Did you shut the window?" I asked curiously, not putting it past him. "No, but I can certainly shut it for you," he said with a sinister sound in his voice. I knew he had some sort of malicious idea, but it was too late for me to figure it out.

Suddenly, the ground rumbled with an intense feeling of dread. Mr Lonely laughed a bit, and with a quick jump, he landed on a train that came upwards and out of the ground! My first thought, after an initial jump of fear, was, "Someone is bound to notice!" I yelled at him to stop, but even before I could finish my sentence, he had travelled to the window, shut its mouth with ease, and then dropped off the train with its sudden but pleasing dematerialization. "I guess we have no time to waste now, hoho!" he exclaimed, as he ran into the woodline.

I quickly followed him, but it seemed that he was going in the direction of whence we initially came from. The only differentiating factor was that we were now disguised by the trees. We returned to the main street shortly after the woodline ended, and stood on the sidewalk, catching our breath through the sharp air of Russie. The buildings were all grey of stone and gloom, with nothing but squares and rectangles as shapes among the places. The snow somewhat showed life, but it ultimately killed the rest of what was left.

No one was outside, and the buildings only seemed to plead for mercy. I looked at Mr Lonely, as we passed buildings that seemed to travel back in time. The architecture went from stone blocks to cabins, and man-made fire to candles of nature. Mr Lonely spoke of how the buildings of squares looked to belong to a notion of the Soviet Union, but he was puzzled as to how it was regressing as we progressed. I offered the idea of it being another doing of the white-cloaked pursuer, and we both agreed it was the most likely.

The town was growing to be unnerving, with fears that seeped into the corners of my vision. Looking back at Mr Lonely, he seemed to be ever so slightly affected as well. I didn't think it was right to mock him, for the air of this changing world was heavy enough to hang a man. The only good notion of this world was that the death of man-made fire seemed to bring a light into man itself; each house had faces within windows. This place was like the memory of someone else, watching this world progress without them.

However, with each regressing house, there were locks of noir hair paired with white, porcelain skin. It was absolutely heart-breaking to see such a calamity in worlds, for what I previously deemed to be like family was now proven to be only a hellspawn. I hoped that in some form, the black and white family was only here to continue the lesson, and not to rob me of my fire. In most thoughts, I prayed to **the great big moon in the sky** that I would not see the woman, and only guide her family to teach her soon. In the end, I just needed more time with her, but now wasn't the moment.

One of the last houses on the street was down a hill, but still standing against the wind. The sign was still unrecognisable, but the sounds weren't. Coming from inside of the small cabin was the sound of a piano being played. Neither of us talked, for we didn't want to break the peculiar peace this world had. Not even the railroad man seemed to want to disturb the music, but there was always the chance of him seeing a different view altogether. There was an aura around the cabin that crashed into one's mindscape almost immediately, but it was all the more intriguing to approach. Was it the white-cloaked figure?

The snow crunching below my feet felt loud enough as it was, and made me feel guilty for such an intrusion, but alas, we had finally found something. I turned to Mr Lonely, and looked to him for an idea. He simply nodded his head, walked around the cabin, and approached it from the side. Hearing the music grow louder was comforting, but still nerve-racking. The increasing sound of music meant the distraction of whoever was inside, but also meant we were growing louder as well.

I decided it would be best if Mr Lonely was the one to look inside for the black and white family, for my mask proved to be rather difficult to manoeuvre near the glass. We traded spots, and with the railroad man taking off his hat, he peered into the window slowly. I awaited his response to tell me everything he saw, but he never seemed to break his gaze. Breaking the gaze meant focusing on the drugging aura of the building. It felt like time had stopped before he finally broke the hourglass, and looked back to tell me what he saw. "There's a young girl playing piano in there, but she didn't have that black hair you mentioned."

I found that it was odd how our piano player seemed to have no relation to the black and white family, yet the power she had that drew us to her evoked nothing but a hellish fear. Such a youthful girl who worked on scales seemingly had the strongest power of evil alongside her black and white keys. When I asked Mr Lonely to quietly describe her appearance, he only mentioned her hair. It was supposedly long and luxurious, with many brown curls and waves that sprung about. It reached down to her back, and seemed to dance along with the music.

Hearing the music still playing, I decided the beak of the mask was worth fighting. I switched places with Mr Lonely, and then looked into the window from the side. The room was seemingly empty, with just her playing the piano. There were pieces of sheet music scattered about, but the one she played was impossible to see from the window. She looked like an angel compared to this world, but her aura was nothing of a holy apparition.

One would assume that her teacher might be present, but there was not another soul within that place. The girl herself had a soul, but it was all the more peculiar to feel the energy she possessed that counterbalanced her horrible aura. Maybe the piano was an escape from it all, and she turned to a composer's tears written in ink. It didn't feel right to stalk someone in grief, but that was what the murder led me to see. Each eye of the crow was on the top of the roof, simply observing what I chose to do next.

I looked away from the window, and turned to Mr Lonely for an idea. He quietly whispered through the mask, "I'd like to see her leave before we advance into the schoolhouse." I agreed with the railroad man, and chose to follow through with it. We awaited her departure from the schoolhouse for a moment's waltz, listening to her never endlessly playing. She only seemed to finish a song when her original audience in the sky had left.

When dusk had arrived, the final chord was diminished. We both watched her get up from her seat, but she never did leave the cabin. She simply disappeared into the air, like waking up from a dream, or a nightmare in this case. The last look I got of her was her ragged dress. She looked to wear the same rags as the man from Room #47, and it broke my poor heart.

Before she completely dissipated, she looked to be humming a soft melody to herself, but none could hear it from the wind's sighs. Never once did she look like she paid mind to this world, and was simply here to learn. Maybe the girl was used to this world, and sought to make it interesting within her own imagination. If it were up to me, I would assume she knew more than a mere bystander, for her dynamics of song were not written as such. She created new emotion with each run-through of the piece, and never once did they repeat.

I felt connected to this girl, in a way that I never felt before. I could see that this was her Hell, and she was longing for a way to escape. I had to fight the tears that formed in my eyes, for I couldn't have Mr Lonely see me in such distress. I didn't think Mr Lonely noticed the girl's connection to Hell in the same way I did, and it was hurtful to think such. I wanted to save her, I truly did, but I could only start with an investigation.

Mr Lonely was the first to approach the door to the schoolhouse, for I was still lost in thought. Neither of us heard or saw the girl lock the door, so it was likely that it was still open for our investigation. The thought of her purposefully not locking it was unnerving, to say the least; it meant the chance of someone else being inside. I felt a fool when thinking of such, but the concept grew in probability, as the schoolhouse still possessed the hellish aura. I regrettably believed the host to be the girl; was I misconstrued?

Upon entering the building, I felt my head spin with a drugging feeling of being back in Hell. Mr Lonely seemed to be affected as well, for his stature seemed to be also dizzy. It was an incredibly overwhelming feeling of dread; one we both experienced before, but never expected to come back, especially in a small schoolhouse in Russie. The inside of the schoolhouse itself was in disarray; all except the piano. I couldn't bring myself to gaze at the ceiling, but judging from the floor, I could assume it was not in its Dimanche best.

I felt myself lose consciousness every time I lingered in the thought of this place, and it led me to leave the schoolhouse rather quickly. There was nothing to see, except for the Russian pieces of sheet music. When Mr Lonely came out of the room, his steps were staggered, as he no longer seemed to glide across the snow. He agreed that there was nothing in there except the personification of true Hell, and it was a damning notion as well. I asked myself how the girl was able to stay conscious in there for such a long time!

If only we knew then and there why the feeling of Hell was conjured. If only we knew why the aura still lingered in the schoolhouse, and if only we knew who the schoolmaster was. If only we knew we were being watched, and if only we knew where from. If only we knew the schoolmaster was above us, and if only we knew our pursuer was as well. If only we knew that the schoolmaster was crouched along the ceiling, studying us like just another note. I beckon thee, one must always **be aware of their surroundings.**

The Snow Will Melt

Neither of us saw where the girl had gone, so we were left once more to walk on our own. From the look of night growing closer, I knew it wouldn't be long before I would come face to face with my mentor. I was anxious to see what the great big moon in the sky had to say to me. The sea of night was coming, and the crows sensed it too. Beginning to walk back to our established house, we began to notice the differences inside each home.

With the absence of the sun, it was easier to see within the houses of the snowy town. Many looked to be eating at tables, while others were fast asleep in preparation for work the next day. One of the last houses, before the point of time changing, looked to be a tavern inside. There were many men and women alike all there together, singing a solemn melody with glasses in hand. While the words were unintelligible, the tune was a universal cry for a need of life, regardless of their black and white appearance.

I expected Mr Lonely to argue his way into a glass of Medovukha, but he seemed distant himself. It appeared that their drinking song appealed to minds all alike. "Don't you want to go in?" I asked him quietly.

"There's no use for such,"

was all the railroad man spoke of the entire way back to the house. It felt ominous to hear him in such a way, for the snow was frosting his mind, as well as my own.

I wondered what was the cause for the sudden change in him, for it seemed to be a gradual shift over time itself. I felt guilty for leading him to such a new mind, but it could also be beneficial with a new set of eyes. Those dolls were not the start of his change, for it was something deeper than just a piece of porcelain. I decided to not let it bother my being for too long, and continued to walk into the undead, square buildings. The more modern side of town was harder to judge inside, for everything was too dim to read; I hoped to never see that poor girl in this place. The railroad man started humming to himself, and singing softly with each step.

"Tell him I'm leaving, tell him I'm gone."

He seemed to be lost in song to himself, never once allowing me to hear the full thing. His glides along the snow changed into dances, as he fully lost himself. I thought his method of handling everything was certainly odd, but it helped him gain his sense of person back, nevertheless; he never seemed to stop the melody playing.

The main street curved up a hill that led to the finer houses, and meant our walk wouldn't be much longer. Deciding to avoid the front altogether, we went through the woodline until we could see our little space we called home temporarily. Worried of Hell following us home, I tried to speak to Mr Lonely once again. "Which way do you want to go inside?" I asked. I was met with momentary silence, until he spoke up in a better mood.

"Let's use the window, but I'm curious to see if there are any eyes on us from the manor. Can you get up there by yourself, or do you need any help?" He asked somewhat teasingly. It was somewhat refreshing to hear his playful side return, for it felt like he had a hidden intention of something pleasing. "I don't suppose I could get up there without your train, so do you have any ideas?" I asked, feeling a faint smile creep across my lips. "Use your fire, maybe you can use it to project yourself upwards; you could join the murder or something."

His idea seemed foolish, but I was willing to give it a try. The house was made of bricks, so it had a chance to fight a rogue flame. However, Hell managed to burn straight through the stone. The railroad man disappeared from sight, as he progressed his way toward the manor window; I trusted that he wouldn't advance any further than just the snowed lawn. Readying myself to emit a controlled flame proved to be harder than I initially anticipated, for the worries of being seen, and possibly burning down the whole place crept alongside my back.

The last time I successfully projected a flame, I did not see the results, or even the fire itself. I was incredibly worried about not being able to control it without the fear of life or death; I felt as if I depended on adrenaline to be my spill. Relaxing my body and flicking my fingertips, I felt the palms of my hands heat up with light. It was easy to summon the fire now, but to truly use it, other than a mere light, was seemingly impossible! Using anger and fear worked, but it didn't fully control it; I needed to master the ability to project flames with an eased mindscape.

It felt wrong to project flames, and the guilt was the worst to overcome. I wish I was as insouciant as Mr Lonely was; maybe I could set something on fire. I felt like a monster when I projected flames onto others, but this wasn't a person. If anything, it was going to help me and my journey following the crows. Reminding myself of my own morals, I finally felt like it was okay to project fire onto something else, even if it was just the snow.

Igniting my hands to a brighter flame, I jumped and projected a flame straight down, as best I could. I felt lightless immediately, but the moment I'd go to look back down, I fell to where I gazed. It took many trials to not look at my feet, but when I gazed straight upwards at the great big moon in the sky, I flew to the point where I could kiss my mentor's feet! I had finally mastered the ability to fly using a projection of fire! Looking down to the window, I fell to its lips.

With a quiet open, I crept into the house, as it creaked under my feet. Sighing into the blankets on the ground, I watched Mr Lonely join me a few minutes later. "I suppose you did it?" He asked me, seemingly proud of my accomplishment. I simply nodded my head in response. I was beyond tired from persistent melting, and all I wanted now was a well-earned rest.

Mr Lonely sat on his blankets upright, and began talking to me, forcing me out of my dozed mindscape. "Before you go to sleep, we need to know what we're planning to do. We know of a girl and a place, but which do we follow?" He asked me while taking off his hat. "If it were up to the crows, they only perched upon the schoolhouse. They never once flocked to the girl," I yawned.

"That makes sense, I guess. We'll head back in the morning to see who all frequents the place."

"If it comes down to it, do you think we'll actually have to fight that little girl?"

"Probably, but I'm not too worried about it. I don't think that girl is responsible for anything other than an incredible performance, hoho!"

"I don't think I could bring myself to hurt her. She's too youthful."

"You won't have to; it should just be our pursuer."

"And if she was ours?"

"Well, then she won't be so youthful anymore."

The conversation was seemingly left at that, and was an ominous way to end the day in whole. I felt content with the progression, but wanted to deny the fact that the girl was likely to die in all of this. Sighing into sleep, I wanted to escape into my dreams,

but my consciousness never left.

Something was keeping me here and awake, and I was growing quite fearful of making confrontation.

I opened my eyes, and saw my mask and hat just as I had left them. The faint smell of herbs was pleasant to visit, but I was worried of another presence enjoying the scent as well. My back faced Mr Lonely; where he lied I could only assume. I had thought that he had gone to bed, but alas, I could have been wrong. Laying still, I listened for anything out of the ordinary, and to my surprise,

I heard something.

There were rolled footsteps coming from behind my back and down towards the stairs. From the angle I laid at, as still as a corpse, I would be able to see who was coming down the stairs in a crack of view between two boxes. It seemed like it took forever for the mysterious person to come down the stairs, but after an excruciating still, my eyes fixated on a form travelling down the stairs. It was certain to be Mr Lonely's, but I questioned his motives. I never heard him open the door or move any boxes; it seemingly looked like he just wanted some privacy. Nevertheless, it was still unrestful, for my consciousness never ceased.

I never did fully trust him, for he never bothered to show his true face, other than when it suited him. He lived a secluded life, even when on the stage of hundreds. I never knew what was behind that mask of his, and it was just as ominous as it was infuriating. How could a man live behind such a mask? What was he afraid of? Questions as such were what managed to keep me up, rather than the coldened floor with not-so-warming blankets. The railroad man was just as mysterious as I first met him, never once failing to keep his identity a secret. It was hard to believe his origins at all!

I could hear him softly humming to himself, and it seemed to not be muffled by any sort. A part of me debated to sneak along the stairs and look at the railroad man unmasked, but I only assumed that it would come in time from **the great big moon in the sky.** Insomnia looked to be the only one upstairs with me now, and it was a bothersome roommate. I forced my roommate to leave my space, and the eviction proved to be successful. Soon, I was drifting off into slumber, and visiting my mentor through my dreamscape once more in the mind of Father Drexel.

I had only the dream of a white void, slowly consuming my stars. It drove me mad with its persistent chase, never ceasing until I exposed my fearful nerves. I could only escape the blanc by flying away in short spurts of flames. It felt like an exasperated test from the white-cloaked figure. However, I was finally cloaked with the clothes of Father Drexel, and it was certainly refreshing to escape the cold. Never once did I see the white-cloaked figure, but I was definitely in fear of getting ambushed by the cannon. In the end, I was awakened by myself being consumed by the blanc void. Our pursuer was growing increasingly livid, and was willing to change forms to reach their end goal.

Although I was humiliated by the consuming void, I was still thankful for the rest. Insomnia no longer saw me as a friend, but it seemed as if my eviction led it to find the railroad man. It was impossible to prove from my dreamscape, but it felt as if he never went to his own. I could do nothing if he had left the house except hope to the crows that they'd watch over him. He had a hunger for the best of others, and he would do anything to achieve it. Nevertheless, he kept some sort of persona with his mask, like a limit to his endless capabilities. I feared what he was capable of, but I had to simply trust it was all in favour. He had a mind of his own that would guide him, and I had to entrust in him to be able to have integrity. The night was a welcoming hour, and I hated to spend it in disarray. For all that it meant, the dismay would not last much longer. I beckon thee, one must always **have faith in thy outcome.**

Missing Confrontations

The squawk of the crows awakened me, and caused my eyes to involuntarily open. I left my blank dreamscape in phases, seeing mixtures of what I perceived to be real and fake colliding with one another. In one instance, I was back at the cathedral, in another, I was against the cold, wooden floor. Did my eyes see smoke, or the mere breath of my soul frosted in the air? I couldn't remember my dream at all from the night's danse, and I began to question if I even dreamed at all. Nevertheless, everything became clear to my consciousness, once I fully sat upright

I noticed that Mr Lonely was upstairs again; he was seemingly collected and ready for me to be as well. I shuddered at the thought of him moving among my unconsciousness, but I decided it was not worth the trouble to confront him about the matter. I wouldn't say that I was fearful, but rather wanted to preserve my blissful ignorance. However, it was hard to ignore the fact of how I was no longer blissful, and seemingly just ignorant. Nevertheless, I suppose that an ignorant man slept better than a man with a conscience.

The railroad man turned to me with a hidden smile, and began to chuckle to himself. "I'm in the mood for some breakfast; are you? *We can go to the big rock candy mountain, hoho!*" I didn't think anything of his maniacal laughter, for he always seemed to find something outright hilarious every hour. However, this time was different than all of the others, for what he laughed at was not an insult or mindless narcissism.

It was a statement of him finding excitement in getting breakfast, and it likely meant going through all matters necessary to simply get a cup of coffee. I knew better than to detest him, for it would end worse for any house that he decided to prey on. "Don't worry too much! As long as they don't see us, then they won't have to deal with us. It will be your fault if I get a new suit, haha!" I cringed at his words, but ultimately knew it would be me that didn't know how to linger in the shadows.

I sighed, questioning why a cup of coffee was worth a spilled kettle of life, but Mr Lonely only saw it as two of the same-sized cups. Neither of us needed kettles or cups, but only the drive of which we were put here. As for Mr Lonely, his drive was always the desire for the better. We descended onto the bottom floor, and moved boxes and decorations out of the way of the door. I put on my mask and hat once more, as the railroad man opened the door to the late morning drift.

The sun was still wrapped in blankets of clouds from the winter, and the house before us was seemingly still asleep. It was a relief to know that not a soul was awake in the manor, but I questioned the duration of the peace. Mr Lonely noticed the silence, and continued to follow in its voice. He opened the back door ever so quietly, and crept inside. The door didn't stay open for me at all, for it wanted to slam immediately onto my fingers!

Terrified of it creaking or shouting out to its owners, I quickly stuck my foot into the doorway, admitting I was now a part of the trespass. Slowly shutting the door behind me, I followed Mr Lonely into the new room. The air was so warm, and the entire house felt welcoming; I felt like I deserved to be executed for disturbing such peace. I entered the building without consulting my mentor, and now I felt as if the act of being caught was an accepting punishment for this crime. I didn't feel favoured at all, for every step against the hardwood floor yelped and cried from my weight.

The room we entered was rather small, but it had other doorways that led to more sections of the house. The ceiling was high, with white paint and many portraits that hung along the walls. There were plants in all of the windows, with translucent white fabric for curtains. What caught my attention the most in this room was the table in the middle of it all.

It was a darkened oak with round edges and chairs surrounding it, but nothing bore its face. The room smelled of coffee, and I knew that meant the adventure might end more suddenly than I had initially anticipated. Mr Lonely rolled his feet into another room, perfectly matching the sounds of the house. When I followed, it revealed itself to be the manor's kitchen. The whole room was filled with chestnut cabinets and white tiles, and assortments of pots and pans scattered about.

Thus, Mr Lonely's mission began, to make himself a satisfying cup of coffee without murdering an entire family. I decided I would watch out for the family, while the railroad man toyed with their belongings. I didn't care about how he made it, but I could hear him effortlessly walking around to take what he needed, all while singing to himself in the process. "On the birds and the bees and the cigarette trees," he seemed to hum to himself. I walked around the corner of the kitchen, and saw how it immediately led to the dining room. The room was massive with cabinets of glassware reaching the ceiling, and a table that I only questioned how they managed to fit its body inside of the room!

I wish I was here under different circumstances, but alas, I was forced to watch for the people who owned such a lavishing home. I wanted to admire the place for its beauty, for the dark carpets matched the table and plant pots perfectly, but I had to be aware of the disturbance of anything within eye or earshot. The dining room seemed to have two openings to other rooms. One looked to connect to a hallway where our original room was, and the other to a family room. That room was the furthest away from what I knew, but oh, how it looked to belong in a cathedral.

Each of the walls had pictures of who I presumed to be the masters of the house, and a piano tucked away into a corner that I couldn't see much of. There were tea cups and luxurious pieces of furniture that all matched with the rest of the interior. I was completely mesmerised by the looks of this house, and I almost forgot about the reason I was there. It wasn't until I heard a door open and shut from above did fear ensue.

I felt my heart jumping out of my chest, and my face beginning to feel dizzy and hot behind my mask!

I quickly turned around to see Mr Lonely's progress on his worthless cup of coffee, and to my relief, it looked to be finally brewing. He poured the coffee out of a kettle, and into a cup I would assume would never return to this place. I sighed quietly to myself, but still felt my nerves grow. Mr Lonely seemed to sense that someone was now awake, and so quieting his voice, he decided to take the cup with him. "Boys, I'm not turning," he quietly hummed. He left the kettle there, as he swiftly walked back outside and into the wintery world.

I was the last to leave the house, but not without a thirst for one last look at the beauty within. The hallway looked back at me; I could see hundreds of rooms across the walls, and a grand staircase facing the front door. The stairs were a beautiful dark oak colour, but with footsteps travelling down its steps! I quickly dashed out of the house as fast as I could! I cared more about getting out of there, rather than being quiet.

The house knew that I didn't belong, and it was doing its best to tell everyone inside that I was not welcome. The fact was not that I wasn't worthy, but I was just with the wrong crowd. This house did not care for people like the railroad man, and it didn't want me to steal a cup as well. I quickly followed Mr Lonely to the side of the house, into the garden and away from view. We knelt under a window that led to the dining room, as we awaited for any signs of us being noticed.

Nothing followed the sound of me shutting the door out back, nothing followed our footsteps that hurried away, and nothing followed the smell of coffee around the garden. However, what we heard was the sound of the front door. Leaving the front porch seemed to sound like a small group of children. I crawled closer to the front of the house, avoiding being seen by windows, and managed to see the children in question. There were three children walking down the road; all three were boys of varying ages, a young child, a young boy, and a young adult. They all wore matching clothes of little black suits and pants, and had matching pure, black hair.

They were easily recognized as children of the black and white family, and their notions matched it. They seemed to be walking in the direction of town, and they never spoke or skipped; only silence and menacing tones matched. I turned to Mr Lonely, who was now behind me and watching as well, and asked his opinion on the matter. He simply just pushed his mask up with a gentle movement, and took a sip of his coffee.

He didn't seem to care about the children, or the act of almost being caught. He only seemed to even recognize my question until after his cup was empty. "I think that this house has terrible coffee, but their cups are nice." I scoffed at his remarks, and couldn't help but roll my eyes. "No, no, think about it, frog.

The coffee is inside the cup, and it's a terrible taste of a bitter void, but the cup itself is quite beautiful. The people inside this house are bitter, but the house itself is a beautiful palace, hoho!" He looked at the cup, and took further notice of its design and intricate engravings. It was white with blue paint depicting flowers and snow together, small words in Russian followed alongside the lip, and almost seemed like it was a trim on a dress. It was certainly beautiful, and Mr Lonely thought so as well; I knew that by the end of the trip, it would be in his cupboard.

"Do you suppose those children are going to school?"

"They ought to be, but we'd have to follow them to find out."

"I don't think I can go, if I was being honest. Just the aura from the schoolhouse alone was enough to make me want to vomit. I just need more time to work on myself."

I had no response from Mr Lonely for an elongated moment. We simply sat in an uncomfortable silence while the snow dug into our feet. I regretted ever speaking of the weakness I felt from the school, and I regretted ever suggesting to separate. I could see him forming words in his head that consisted of insults and a value of, "You can only grow from exposure," but they never left his mouth. Finally, the silence broke with him humming.

"I'll go and watch the schoolhouse for anything notable. If something is urgent, *listen for a jingle, a rumble, or a roar*. I want you to be able to project flames on command, and consistently propel yourself when I get back. Do whatever it takes. If you can't by the time I get back, we'll do it my way."

I nodded my head, feeling slight relief from his agreement, but still felt uneasy from the concept of not being able to find progress in my betterment. I was worried of my mentor not allowing me to do such, for the crimes I committed with Mr Lonely were done against my better judgement. I simply hoped that the crows would be willing to help, and the most severe that my punishment would be was to not be able to project a flame on the first try. I watched Mr Lonely walk towards the woodline, and begin his pursuit in stalking the children to school. I was nervous about what he would do without a witness, but I suppose he would do it regardless if he chose to, with or without me.

I was left alone beside the house, in a frost of crunched snow. Not knowing where to go to practise my endurance, I looked for my crows to give me a sign. It was pleasing to my person to see them again, and pleasing to my soul to follow them once more. They weren't perched on a tree or lying still on a shingle, but flying swiftly towards the hills behind the manor. I quickly followed them, no longer caring if I was seen from the inside of the window.

They led me quite a ways before they rested on a branch. We were beyond the manor, beyond our house, and to a flattened hillside past a group of trees with a small path looping around. There looked to be a frozen lake in the middle of the circled pathway, and manmade structures tucked away in various corners of the lake. It was in my best interest to follow the path around the lake, and to learn from my mentor in the process. I looked for my mentor around the lake, and to my surprise, the moon stood before me right in the middle of the sky!

I never knew of the moon at day; it made me feel honoured in a sense. I had not an audience of stars, but just a private meeting with the moon. Looking at my options of either going to the left or the right, I chose to travel towards the left. The right was on a higher plateau of sorts, and only seemed suiting for an ending stride. My left looked to be a narrowing twist of dips into hills.

I began my walk towards the left, and walked down the path that seemed to never make up its mind as to where it wanted to be. There were clearly flatter surfaces that would be better suited for a walk, but the path never seemed to take them. It finally seemed to find itself when we were a quarter of a ways around the lake. The next quarter was extremely flat, with open spaces and remnants of manmade structures. I decided that this would be where my first practice would be held.

One thing about this place was the absurdity of white that engulfed every being. Nothing rested here, for everything stung with a vicious chill of blanc. It was difficult to focus, but I pushed myself in honour of my mentor visiting me. I stepped off of the path, and into an open area. The treeline was a fair distance away, so it ensured me to know that I would not burn down the forest.

I was by myself in an open field of snow, with it nipping away at my coldened body. Between the smell of faint blueberry hibiscus tea, and the sounds of the wind dancing, I felt collected enough to begin. I raised my hand in front of me, and cast a flame to my fingertips. Despite the wind roaring against my hand, my fire never ceased. I took pride in the undying flame within me, but now I needed to channel it outwards.

I looked for a distant target to practise aiming at, and the only thing that came to view was the remnants of an old man-made cabin. Only a wall stood obliged to meet me, and even then, it seemed to be in misery from the absence of family, and bearing piles of snow. It was only right for me to practise against its body, for I could bring it the peace that it ever-so craved. I raised my arm towards the wooden wall, and decided to take a new approach to projection. Perhaps the notion of projecting my body will allow the flames to mimic me and travel off of my body?

I began pressing my fingertips against the back of my thumb in a tight manner, building up the power behind a flick. When I felt ready enough, I tried flicking my fingertips towards the wall in a straight manner. The white burned brighter, for I had finally managed to project a flame across a plain calmly! Watching the wooden wall burn to its last log was satisfying in knowing that it was controlled. I was satisfied here, and chose to continue the lesson elsewhere.

I walked along the path, letting the flames die out within my hands. I seemingly reached halfway around the frozen lake when I saw another man-made structure. There was a small bridge that crossed a narrow section of the lake, and it looked to be directly under the moon's gaze. Walking along the curved boards, I looked at my mentor in the sky, and couldn't help but smile. I thanked him for his patience and allowance, and meditated for a moment longer.

Closing my eyes was relieving, for the harsh white no longer pierced my eyes like a jagged knife. I was with the sound of wind, and let it gently push me along. The scent of herbs was easier to smell with no vision, and it felt more endearing in a sense. Sitting with the moon allowed tranquillity to join the wind, and slowly readied me to continue. After a long moment of peace, I slowly opened my eyes, and felt it was ready to keep my feet moving.

The path was heading uphill, and was becoming thinner against a drop-off to the lake. There were many dead limbs of dried trees that scratched at my legs along the path, but it was easy enough to step over them. As the path seemed to go downhill once more, the limbs went away, and allowed me to walk down with ease. The cold trail was beginning to twist with trees covering both sides, causing the world to get colder. I felt like a trial was before me, and the thought of seeing nature hide me was unnerving.

I looked around for any sign from the moon, but all my eyes saw was white with black streaks of a tree's rough skin. Among the floor, however, was a noticeable foot trail. The snow was packed in, leading beyond the trees, and off of the path entirely. I didn't know if it was a sign to take the strange trail, but if many others before me made the decision to do so, it may be a sign to do so as well. One could argue in the same sense that it was a sign to go against the herd, but I had to trust that **the great big moon in the sky** allowed me to see the trail for a reason.

Walking the new path was difficult, for the combination of a steep hill with iced foot tracks proved to be more difficult than I had initially anticipated. I was swallowed by trees and ice, with my beak beginning to get caught in hanging arms of wooden flesh. I felt my hands getting scratched by invisible twigs, as I used them as guides along the path.

The moon was invisible from here, and I couldn't help but feel as if I had made a grave mistake. Nevertheless, it would only be more treacherous to go downhill from here.

In the distance, it seemed to finally level out, but not without a final notion of a thickened line of bushes and trees. Pushing through what felt like a nail of Hell, I persevered to the other side of the bushes. Feeling like I had climbed out of the womb, I made it to a seemingly new world. It was an open field in its wintery whole! There were no bushes, thorns, limbs, or a single tree in sight from here, but just an open field of pure, rich snow.

This place was untouched by man; no one made it past the thorns. In the sky, as clear as day, its cherished skin created the portrait of the moon congratulating me on my find. I fell to my knees, and laid down to look at the sky at a new angle. I took off my mask and hat, and watched the moon's smile fade in and out with each passing gust of wind. The snow cried on my hair, dampening it with my weight alongside its face.

I felt like I had achieved ultimate peace, and that my head was as clear as the snow before me. The aura of evil could no longer affect me, for the bite of frost and the sting of fire were both on my side. In the same sense, it finally felt as if I could think properly as well. I no longer hid from the thought of the black and white family, or my thoughts of the woman herself. I loved her, but whoever the white cloaked figure was, regardless of their face, needed to be stopped; I would not let Hell's torment outlive me.

Sitting up, I dusted off the pile of snow that had formed on my coat and other belongings. When I looked in the distance beyond the plain, I saw more buildings matching the changing architecture of this town. One that spoke to me in particular was the building closest to the plain, for it spoke with the strongest voice, and looked to be a bass in the choir.

Deciding to travel there with Mr Lonely, I stayed put on the plain, and continued my meditation with the moon. I had reached my highest point, and now I had no plans of travelling higher. The only goal now was to descend and help others travel my same feat. I rested with the moon, until I was covered with stars and snow. Only then did I decide to go down the steep hill to the clearway.

Walking through icy thorns downhill was impossible at this hour, so I felt the need to challenge myself in finding another way. The idea of using my flames to join the sky to the clearway seemed to be the best idea, for I was growing cold myself, and wanted to kiss my mentor's feet. Putting back on my mask and hat, I started to run towards the woodline. Flicking my fingertips towards the ground, I jumped and projected fire at the snow. In an instance, my feet were no longer being bit by frost, and were lightless, as I glided over trees in a heated bliss!

I pushed my arms down to give me a small boost, and glided down to the back of the manor with a smile as big as my mentor's. I let the flames flicker out, as I landed on the roof of the manor. I walked along the roof and sat on the top ledge, waiting for Mr Lonely's return. I didn't need to check the small house for his presence, for his person would not allow him to rest there for other reasons than sleep. Up on the roof, I could see practically everything, and I knew Mr Lonely would envy a place like this.

Like a moth to a flame, I could see him return to the manor close to the moon's full hour. He seemed to almost immediately notice me, and grew envious. However, he never once attempted to pursue the spot. Instead, he simply walked around back, and into our house. I decided to join him, so we could catch up with each other's new discoveries.

Upon gliding up to the window, and climbing inside, I noticed that something about Mr Lonely seemed different. It wasn't his attitude or voice, but rather his appearance. It was too dark to fully see, but I knew it would be revealed at some point. He sat on the top step, as I studied him from behind. Shutting the window behind me, I patiently waited for him to speak first.

"You seem more comfortable with your fire, I'm guessing you earned *the sugar in your tay?*"

"Yes, I feel as if I have reached my highest, and I feel ready to foresee Hell's end"

"We'll need to put that to the test tomorrow then."

He stood up and faced me, and that was when I immediately noticed what was different with him.

His coat was now different; it was black and slick.

It looked to belong to the same variety of the children who left for school, but did they ever return? I didn't know when or if they ever came back to the house, but I knew that I couldn't trust Mr Lonely's answer. He seemed to notice my uneasiness, and looked as if he was preying on it.

"What's wrong, Drexel? You look as if *your pay was docked for the time you were up in the sky.*"

"...I just can't help but notice your new coat."

"My apologies, I was getting quite cold watching children playing piano and getting slapped on their wrists; I wanted something warmer. Next time, I'll get you one as well."

"There shouldn't be a next time."

The railroad man simply laughed in response. He could clearly dig the hole deeper if he chose to, but he never did. Instead, he simply sat down on his blankets, and leaned back with a sigh. I was furious with him, for it felt like not knowing where his coat came from was worse than knowing. I didn't quite know how to approach it anymore, due to exhaustion and a dollop of fear, but I wanted him to know that he wasn't as sneaky as he once thought.

I turned to him without a second thought and spoke, "Wear it all you want, I see through your mask. You're just as bad as the white cloaked figure." I turned away from him before he could respond, allowing me some sort of peace between us. Because of him potentially murdering a man, or even a student, our mission here fell between the lines of success and failure. It made no sense for him to commit such an idiotic act either, for his revenge shined brighter than my vengeance.

He never made sense to me, for everything seemed calculated, yet improvised. I wanted so badly to tear off his mask, and see how the man could deal with his true flesh. He did nothing but hide it through mindless acts of selfishness and cruelty. Nevertheless, I wanted the night to aid my temper, and hopefully resolve within the stars as well.

I no longer trusted the railroad man; even the small cent of worth it had was completely spent. Between his secretive being and his careless decisions, I couldn't stay here a minute longer. Without assurance from him, I had no choice but to confront the school house the next day immediately. Despite the new coat bringing a new dire feeling, I felt a notion of pride in that I could withstand more now than I ever could before. Thanks to **the great big moon in the sky** and the crows, it would appear to have worked out within the end of the night. I was a man of Fire, and was willing to burn our pursuer through Winter, no matter who was under the cloak. I beckon thee, one must always **fight the urge to succumb to the cold.**

Her Concierto

Morning arose, but neither did I or Mr Lonely. Both of us simply laid on the ground, not wanting to accept that Day had already come. I could hear the railroad man humming to himself, "*Filly me oo-ree aye-ree ay*"; his little melody seemed to be the only thing to keep him awake. He had his new coat on him like a blanket, and it angered me with how comfortable he seemed with it. Regardless of how I felt, I kept reassuring myself it was all in the moon's favour, so that I wouldn't burn him alive.

It wasn't until I met Mr Lonely did I feel these levels of anger and dismay. He was a disease that plagued my faith and life, and always managed to make me betray my mentor. I never quite knew how to perceive him, but as this day progressed, I simply decided to know him as only his name. It mattered not who he was and what he valued, but only of what Hell had in plans for this town. Sitting up, I looked at the railroad man, and saw that he had done the same before me, singing to himself the same, "*Filly me oo-ree aye-ree ay.*"

I had no dreams from last night, for the white-cloaked pursuer seemed to sense that I was hunting them. It caused me to have blank dreamscapes, with or without caring about what Mr Lonely did after dark; what he chose to do no longer bothered me. We spoke of nothing to each other, and simply got ready to head into town. The humming could have been in spite, a challenge to see who broke first, or just a distant reality of the end coming. I felt like it was a combination of all three, but the distant reality was approaching closer with each passing string of song. I sighed, as I made my way to the door downstairs with Mr Lonely.

Today felt different in a way that I only experienced one other time, but I was not gifted the recollection of such just yet. After leaving the house, the land of snow seemed to have a thicker brightness than usual, and the sky seemed bluer than most paintings would depict. The sun was up to something, but I had no clue as to what it would be. The mischievous sun didn't seem to bother the railroad man, for his tune never ceased.

"*Filly me oo-ree aye-ree ay,*" he kept chanting, "*Filly me oo-ree aye-ree ay.*"

I will admit that his tune was infecting me, for I began to pick up on the lyrics, and hum and sing along with him.

With what I first deemed to be mockery was now a ballad between us, and made me feel less angry. I felt motivated to walk faster into town, and felt a surprising notion of no longer caring if we were seen. I couldn't help but smile with each line of the song, causing me to skip alongside Mr Lonely. Leaving the manor's gates from the front was somewhat thrilling, feeling connected with the railroad man finally. I danced in step with him, as we continued to grow stronger in voice, "*Filly me oo-ree aye-ree ay.*"

He clicked his heels together, and looked at me with a satisfying notion of letting me understand him. It was incredibly surreal to feel this empowered, but song was his crow, and a medley can work a tarrier. We walked into town, like we were the owners of such, and began to skip along the slick, whitened snow. I never felt my ankles grow cold from the frost; I blamed it on the new heartbeat of step. There were crows far ahead of us, and it was exhilarating to know that singing alongside the railroad man was in favour of the moon.

It was magnificent to see how songs united hearts together, despite differences all around. I felt as if I should see Mr Lonely as something more than his name, and maybe a man that works by melody. As the architecture seemed to change back to the old memories of Russie, the song we sang experienced a sudden key change. I didn't follow immediately, and neither did Mr Lonely.

Before us was the schoolhouse, and through the window was only one child, and a distinct trail of footprints into the woodline behind. It looked to be the same girl from the last time I was here, but she was being closely observed by her schoolmaster. I couldn't see who the schoolmaster was, but the clothes that they wore were as familiar as the mischievous sun. Mr Lonely was the first to approach the window; he went from the side of the building once more, and looked inside. After only a mere second of looking in, he immediately turned to me with a sense of urgency.

"Drexel, look into the schoolhouse, and to the schoolmaster. I don't think the girl is the one with the aura."

I hesitated for a moment, but I knew that I would be the only one to recognize the faces of the black and white family. I traded places with the railroad man, and crept towards the window, with the side of my beak against the glass. At first, I only saw the woman. I felt my heart skip a beat, as it made the choice to enter the room without thinking of anything else. Thankfully, my mind beat my heart to the door, and allowed me to keep my cover to further investigate the schoolmaster.

At a second glance, I could see no resemblance to my woman. The schoolmaster wasn't pure at all, for she had faint wrinkles, a furrowed brow, and an evil notion within her aura. However, when I chose to let my other senses investigate, I could hear my woman's voice as clear as the night sky. She spoke in Russian to the girl, and with her voice growing louder, so did the aura of the building.

I felt nauseous from the schoolmaster, but I couldn't admit that she was the woman from the black and white family. Maybe it was best for me to never reconcile it, for I wouldn't feel as guilty when I ultimately put an end to the white-cloaked pursuer's torment. No, I would never properly defeat Hell if I pretended I only saw the sheep and not the wolf. That schoolmaster had to be the woman from the black and white family, no matter how pure she seemed to be!

However, it did not make sense to me how she looked to be so much older, and frightening, to say the least. Her bun and matching black dress took away her youth, and her face was ageing with grief. I almost didn't want to believe it was her, but the voice was undoubtedly the woman's. It broke my heart to see these worlds collide, but I was here to put an end to Hell. The way her personality had shifted so much only reminded me of the white-cloaked figure.

Our pursuer walked with an ambition of theft, drugs, and murder. This woman walked the same, and oh, how it hurt me to see that poor girl trapped with such a schoolmaster. The woman's purity was no more, and neither was her family's as well. I felt betrayed and lied to, and it made me livid! In the same moment, I could see how the woman was the pursuer, schoolmaster, and even a tattered demon all at the same time! I was amazed how she still found the composure to withstand a human form without her ragged skin exposed!

I always wanted to give someone the benefit of the doubt, that maybe with time they would become better. However, she lost less and less of her purity, and I could see the tattered demon at last. I shuddered at the thought of seeing such a creature again, but I was more livid at the thought of someone else going through my torment. The girl was paralyzed with fear, like I was long ago. I needed to help her, rescue her, save her!

Mr Lonely seemed to notice my quick change of heart, for I felt a sudden hand grab the back strap of my mask and yank me backwards rather harshly. I fell on my back, and looked up to Mr Lonely with anger in my eyes, but I knew he did it for the greater good. I felt my anger cool off with the snow, and then I slowly returned to my feet while out of view from the window. I could see Mr Lonely wanted confirmation that I recognised the schoolmaster to be a tormentor from Hell, so I simply returned the silent nod.

Neither of us knew what to do in the moment, but to charge head-on wasn't the solution; there was something we didn't know just yet, and it would be futile to plan without it. Mr Lonely listened through the wall at what the schoolmaster yelled, but most of it was nonsensical Russian. However, one word was the perfect cognate we needed: concert.

The girl was to perform a concierto? It was impossible to have one in the tiny schoolhouse, so the concept of having it elsewhere was the only other way to let the performance commence. After thinking back to all of the buildings I saw, only one of them looked to be worthy of a concierto performed by a rarity. Back through the street, behind the manor, and beyond the lake was a massive building that was worthy of such a performance. Mr Lonely seemed to agree when I spoke of the place, and so it was settled to go there.

Neither of us wanted to risk being confronted in the open town, for we both felt that the schoolmaster could easily stain the snow. The concert house offered hiding, and more time to prepare. Mr Lonely pulled me away from the window, knowing I would lose my temper if I were to stay any longer. He grabbed me by the arm, and gently dragged me behind the building. The yells could still be heard from even farther away, and it made me feel like the man from Room #47 being dragged away by doctors.

The sudden wave of emotions began to cause me much dismay, and I began to shake with violent convulsions. Mr Lonely went from trying to comfort me to immediately pacifying me, with a quick, efficient hit to the back of my head. I just wanted to save the girl, I just wanted out of Hell, I just needed more tim..

I woke up inside one of Mr Lonely's train cabins.

My initial thoughts were calm and collected, thinking of Mr Lonely's hospitality. Then, the bliss ended abruptly, as I was met with dismay when I realised that I was on a train, knowing Mr Lonely conjured one in town!

I quickly got out of bed and dashed into the next room over, just to see Mr Lonely singing a new melody to himself. The sounds of the iron beast's teeth grinding matched the tempo of the railroad man's new song, and seemingly felt like the locomotive was trying to sing along. My intrusion didn't stop either of their songs, for they progressed with my door slam blending into the melody. Mr Lonely never looked at me, even when I sat directly across from him, he only seemed to look through me at the locomotive. He just continued to sing, *"He was going down the grade making 90 miles an hour,"* never ceasing to answer what I had asked. The only one to answer me was the whistle of the iron beast!

His refusal to talk to me was frustrating, but it caused me to listen to his melody, and found myself becoming relaxed. *"He was found in the wreck with his hands on the throttle, scalded to death by steam."* Feeling as if I was meant to never receive an answer, I sighed, and looked outside of the window. It was still the infamous, blinding hue of white, but it felt better knowing that we were still in Russie. I hoped that the railroad man was just taking a shortcut to the concert hall, and it proved to be so after Mr Lonely finished his song. Ending on a pretty note, the iron beast seemed to cease, and out the door the railroad man went. I followed him, thanking both him and the crows for the small break, but I was still concerned about the girl and her schoolmaster.

Mr Lonely wasn't blind; he immediately pulled me out of thought with a simple, "Stop worrying about it. We can only help if you let go for now and focus." I nodded in agreement, but the thought of that girl's cries still loomed over my head. We both looked at the building before us, and its massive size with intricate carvings. It seemed to have known better days, but alas, the show had to go on.

The building was completely made of a dark grey stone, with columns supporting the outlandishly high roof. The doors were in the front, and looked to be a dark, finished wood. There was not a single ounce of colour on the outside of the building, but upon pushing the creaky doors open, the place roared with its trapped echo, like it was welcoming us into its jaws. The first room upon entering was a fair size, with a stairwell on each side, and a small booth in the front. The carpets were coloured with the familiar crimson red, and its walls were an off-white cream.

The booth matched the doors, with a dusty cash register, and a sign in Russian alongside the border. There were doors on both sides of the booth in equal temperament, but neither of us decided to enter them. Walking up the stairs that groaned with our weight, the air seemed to grow colder with mould and grain. Mr Lonely was in front of me, and he seemed to take the blows of decay harder than I did, for he began coughing, as we entered the balcony area. I thought it was strange to see the railroad man cough up such a fit, but the new place was getting to my head as well; I thought I could see fixtures of monsters alongside the walls, and demons from Hell outside the windows.

We left the balcony in a rush, not wanting to spend too much time in one place. The higher areas were beginning to mess with us, and the urge to descend was increasing. Exiting the balcony led us to a hallway with doors on one side. When Mr Lonely opened them up, it seemed to be a room of only a stained, crimson curtain. The railroad man pushed back the curtains, and to my bewilderment, he made no further advancement.

He slowly raised his arm, without breaking focus of the other side of the curtain, and motioned me to come towards him. A part of me didn't want to listen to his hand's voice at all, for his tensed stature was unnervingly still. Nevertheless, I hesitantly approached the curtain, and upon drawing it back myself, I could see clear as day what was so worthy of silence. We knew this place was a concert hall, but nothing could prepare us for the colossal wonders of the auditorium itself. This was a place that the Cathedral of Flames could be related to, for her beauty looked to match my own in Francia.

The pure white ceiling seemed to reach the moon's feet, without a single look of mould, but many few begrudging cracks. The walls had accompanying Corinthian columns matching with the same emotions, and the floor had a perfect crimson carpet to match the main curtain. The hundreds of thousands of rows of chairs were all a deeply finished oak, and the new world seemed to smell of a forest. The stage was black with a reddened wood finish, but it still managed to resemble a dancing forest. The air was twirling, not necessarily from wind, but just twirling by itself in the camaraderie of frost.

I watched as Mr Lonely approached the edge of the box, and seemed to lower his gaze to the floor. It was an oddity, to say the least, to see a man ignore the beauty in front of him to gaze at the floor. Hanging before him was a grand chandelier that seemed to be in somewhat of a good condition. However, it was impossible to truly judge a silent chandelier; I wanted to see it in its full flame, before I made the call. When I approached the railroad man, he made no remark, except stepping onto the railing of the box. I gasped and rushed towards him, worried of him falling, but he beat me to the confrontation when he simply sang to himself,

"Alright boys, everybody get ready, come on down here, come on boys."

He slowly bent backwards, testing his limits without falling. Then, in a swift movement, he sprung upwards, and he dove off of the railing, gracefully falling to the ground. As expected, the railroad man landed on his feet, and even bowed to his audience, but not without beckoning me to follow him off of the rails. The sun barely lit up the room, but I could still see Mr Lonely motioning me to jump with his hands, almost like a taunt of some sort. I didn't want to jump at all, but the weight of the mould was slowly starting to make me fall uncontrollably towards the railing.

In need of some sort of relief, I climbed on top of the railing, pulling the curtain for support and an aid in my terrible balance. I exhaled slowly, allowing my nerves to calm themselves, and then hoped that the crows would guide me down. Flames were of no use inside of this building, so I had to simply rely on having faith in my ability to land on my feet while rapidly descending. I knew I could do it, for I did with the snow, but not a single blanket of blanc was there to comfort my fall on my back. Knowing it was now or never, I bent my knees, let go of the curtain, and jumped off of the rails!

Falling was an intensely drugging feeling, for everything fell by so fast, yet so slow. I could see the chandelier chasing my gaze downwards, and it caused me to panic. I flailed my arms and legs, sending me spiralling downwards. However, in a sudden notion of clarity, I remembered that I needed to land with my feet first; I quickly stopped flailing, and levelled my feet to the ground. Only in the right form did I hit the ground, and felt the shock of such force shooting up my legs. It was unbearable, and it sent me bending over searching for relief.

I could finally breathe again, but I still felt dizzy, and just plain sick now. I closed my eyes in a need of rest, yet I could still hear the claps and cheers of Mr Lonely. *"Oh boy, you can line 'em,"* cheered the railroad man. I groaned in response, slowly feeling my body detoxify from every pain and sickness. It took a moment of silence for me to properly heal, but alas, I was grounded.

I looked at Mr Lonely for what he chose to do next, and the only thing that seemed to be on his mind was the stage itself. I was confused for a minute, but then quickly realised what the railroad man was up to. Mr Lonely asked me with a hinted smile to his voice, "There's a lot more behind the stage than one would expect; would you care to explore?" I nodded, feeling a sense of curiosity to see what was behind the curtain. The exploration within this building helped me feel better about the girl's concierto, for I felt like us knowing the building would allow us to have an unexpected advantage.

Stepping onto the stage, past the orchestra pit, we looked around to see anything in particular. There were two doors in the back corners, past the drapes, and both of them led to a hallway. It was completely dark and almost impossible to see past one's furthest fingertip, but the flames of the crow were an easy solution to the puzzle. I gently lit a flame within my hand, and traded places with Mr Lonely down the hall. I began leading us down what felt like a maze of corridors, trying to trick me into never escaping. It was off-putting inside of the hallway, to say the least, for every step I took was loosely mimicked by the railroad man, and I'd forget where he was in relation to me.

Everything felt like a guess in here, whether it was doors leading to dressing rooms, or the pace at which Mr Lonely walked. Despite all of the fearful distractions, never once did my flame cease. However, when near the end of the hallway, and past the final door, my flame flickered from the wind pushing against it. How peculiar that the door on the end flickered with wind!

I opened the door, ready to see an open window or an echoing voice, but nothing came out of the room. Stepping inside with Mr

Lonely behind me, the room roared with worse echoes than the hallway. My flame faintly illuminated the ground, and revealed the ground to descend into a staircase. I looked back to Mr Lonely to see if he noticed, and judging from his hollow mask looking downwards, I figured he had. We slowly walked down the stairwell, trying to limit how loud our footsteps were within.

The further we descended, the more my flames seemed to flicker and shake. It was growing unstable with each step, and managed to reach its peak with the final step. The ground became flat, and allowed us to travel towards the new door. Placing my hand on the doorknob to open, I felt uneasy and dreadful. My flame picked up on the feeling as well, and began to fade away in small spurts.

Mr Lonely stepped forward, and with a gentle, yet forceful movement, he opened the door for me. Inside was a void, and it completely swallowed my light. I could hear Mr Lonely shuffle towards the entrance, and then walk through the doorway. "I want a light, Drexel," Mr Lonely said with a hint of frustration in his voice. I sighed at his demand, trying my best to ignite once more, but it proved to be more difficult than I had initially thought.

"It's not working."

"What do you mean it's not working? You're Father Drexel, damn it, get a hold of yourself!"

"I'm trying, believe me, but something is keeping me from igniting."

"It's your own mind, frog. Stop being afraid of the dar-"

A light turned on. Not a light of mine, but a mechanical ignition above our heads. The ceiling lit up with white lights strung around in bulbs, and revealed us to be underneath the stage. However, the whole world felt different, for there was a rumble in the walls, and likely meant outside as well. I turned to Mr Lonely, who was focused on a hatch leading to the stage with a small staircase, and looked for his opinion.

He was silent, no longer humming to himself his little work medley. The rumble in the walls began to grow more ferocious, as people's voices seemed to arrive as well. We looked at each other for any clue as to what to do next, for the concierto was beginning to start.

There was a pause in the commotion, when a familiar voice seemed to be right above our heads speaking in Russian. It was too old to be the girl, so it had to have been that blasted schoolmaster!

We waited for her to end her muffled speech, when a round of applause boomed throughout. Then, footsteps approached the staircase, and walked along the stage. The shuffling above our heads seemed to stop when the aching creak of a small seat being sat on was audibly heard right above the hatch. Mr Lonely climbed the small staircase to catch a glimpse of who was on stage, but after a brief pause of him looking through the crack of the door, he looked at me and faintly nodded. Just from the silent notion, I knew too well that it had to be the girl.

Before I had time to reconcile everything, the first note rang throughout the entire building. It was graceful in its element, yet ghastly in its soul, and it reminded me of the coldened ice rink all the time ago. The girl was to perform in front of her judges, and we were no better than bone skates. I could hear her put her life into each peddled note, as it became clear that her life truly depended on it. It was sickening to be forced to watch the metal cut and watch the ice bleed out, for I wanted no part in it, other than to end the concierto in full.

Mr Lonely noticed my dismay, for he crept closer towards me, and silently ushered me to the stairwell. He whispered into my ear, "We could take her inside the train and then fight everyone, if you want." I didn't know exactly what to say, but the idea seemed better than watching her be murdered. Judging from between the cracks of view, it looked as if the piano the girl played would block us from being seen for just the right amount of time we needed. I couldn't bring myself to be the first one up there; Mr Lonely was the one to open the door for us, on the deal that I bring a fire to burn Hell itself.

When the hatch was fully open, we were both blinded by the light that charged at us like a madman. It took a minute of clarity to see again, but what Mr Lonely saw couldn't have been good. He snapped his head around to face me, and shook his head viciously. When I looked to see what he was fearful of, I saw it as well. Beyond the stage, hidden by curtains, and etched in stone, were cracks scattered about the ceiling and walls puking smoke! I beckon thee, one must always **be ready to hold their breath!**

The Charring

The air was increasingly becoming harder to breathe in, for my nerves and the foreign smoke were working against me. I was lightheaded, and felt my head spinning, yet every time I was to fall backwards, I'd feel a harsh push on my back from Mr Lonely. The girl seemed to be aware of the smoking stage, and her tempo became ever-so-slightly faster. It was a race to finish the movement, but the race couldn't be noticed. None of us were allowed to cough, for it would ruin the illusion that the black and white family worked so hard to achieve.

The smoke began to cloud my vision, and slowly overtook the scent of blueberry hibiscus. I was desperately thinking of some sort of way to save her, but the only way was to kidnap her! I leaned over to Mr Lonely, and whispered to him, "When the smoke covers us, we should take her through the trap door." The railroad man seemed to like the new proposition, and agreed to follow through with it. As we awaited the perfect phrase to abruptly steal the show, we noticed that the ceiling itself began to make noises of groans and whispers.

It wouldn't be long until the ceiling would collapse; the option of taking our chances was becoming increasingly probable. When the point of no longer being able to see the ceiling in total had arrived, that was when Mr Lonely decided to make the move. However, before he could make it to the stage, the inevitable, heart-shattering sound of the ceiling falling in came crashing down! Mr Lonely rushed to save the girl, but I could only see the tails of his coat flap out of sight. The sound of a dying piano shook the entire stage, and so did the blanket of dust and debris that enveloped upon the escapees.

There was a loud slam, and then the absence of light in total. I could hear the girl thrashing around in the railroad man's grip, but she never broke loose. She cried words in Russian that neither of us understood, but all that mattered in that moment was to escape the stage with the girl. Mr Lonely quickly yelled at me to cast a flame, and with a panicking mindset, I quickly ignited my hands. I chased behind them as fast as I could into the stairwell once more, but not without hearing the angry yells and screams of the black and white family.

I was fearful in my step, and only wanted to make sure we were not being followed. Turning back before I shut the door, I lit up the room with a brighter flame. To my horror, it looked as if the hatch was being opened! My nerves acted for me, and I projected the colossal flame straight towards our pursuers! Before I could even comprehend what I had done, I was already running out of the room, slamming the door behind me.

Every time the girl cried out for help, I could hear the railroad man's echoing yells telling her to be silent. He was becoming unintelligible; our language was ripping apart. He began to yell in guttural tones with harsh ending words, and screaming in German. It seemed to somewhat pacify the girl, not in the sense of his tone, but in the notion that it wasn't Russian. We both hurriedly stomped up the stairs, with the railroad man holding the girl over his shoulder.

I was now in the lead, guiding the way by fire up the stairs and back into the hall. The drowning sounds of our echoing stomps were met with a mimicking pair of the black and white family. Opening up the door to the hall, I could see a single outline at the end of the hall, family approaching us. I didn't have time to react or notice anything else, for Mr Lonely swiftly traded places with me, and in turn, handed me the girl. I sat her on the ground to let her stand, and firmly, but gently held her hand, while we watched the railroad man make the next move.

In a blink of a flickering eye, I saw his legs meet the ceiling's air in a flip, before the loud sounds of a train came echoing through the hall. In the same minute, what was a dark hallway was lit up with the train's light and the screams of a Russian. The train disappeared as quickly as it came, seemingly escaping into another room. He quickly kept walking, telling me to hurry along. I never thought I'd have to walk a child into a smear of blood; I hoped to **the great big moon in the sky** that she couldn't see it, due to the lack of light.

Every time the hallway was met with another Russian, Mr Lonely spared no time to send them to Hell by the iron beast. I could feel the girl's hand tighten around me each time the train screamed into the deafening hallway, for she thought she was the one deserving of such. I couldn't take the railroad man anymore; I gently took the girl by the hand and pulled her away into one of the rooms until the coast was clear. Inside the completely darkened room, I made sure to never let go of the girl's hand, but still allowed her the cushion of assurance. The dark was a swallowing entity, and so was this family; I never wanted her to feel trapped again.

Even in the sense of silence, it felt like she understood. She may not like the way it unfolded, but she understood our intentions were far less grim than the black and white family, aside from Mr Lonely's lust for revenge. I lit up the room faintly with another flame, just to let us properly see each other. With the gratitude of the crows, I was able to see the girl's curly locks of brown hair that gently rested among her forehead and down her back, and her beautiful blue dress that completely contrasted her rags. Her eyes were amber with a hint of fear, but as I revealed my own eyes to her by pushing my mask up gently, it seemed to relax her.

When I tried to speak to her, she didn't seem to understand any words I spoke. Only when I placed her hand on my chest and introduced myself as Father Drexel, I noticed that something began to turn within her mindscape. She took my hand and placed it on her arm, and spoke for the first time,

"I am Opus."

I was surprised by her name, but finally felt the connection between us, and felt any previous aura of evil vanish. The moment was pure, and from that point in time, we understood the goal of getting out of there alive no matter the cost.

The sounds of oncoming trains, the terrified screams of others, and the laughs and stomps of Mr Lonely broke the moment we shared, and pulled us back into the hallway. I could hear the railroad man yelling for me in a German accent; it was better than before, but still unnerving. He quickly picked up the pace and slammed the door open to the stage, and let us in front. The concert hall was exploding with debris and fire, and it caused me to panic. I felt like I had no choice but to grab Opus, and try to fly over the burned faces and detached ligaments!

I pushed off of the ground with my feet catching fire, and carried Opus with me. She never once looked down before us, but I could still see the railroad man enjoying every moment of dodging the life-ending perils. I hastily landed to push open the doors leading outside, and quickly ushered the girl out of the Corinthian columns' way. Mr Lonely made it out of the building without a sparing second, before the building rumbled and began to collapse onto its knees. When the concert hall finally died, I finally rested in the fact that I saved Opus, and that she could finally see the great big moon in the sky for herself.

The building's demise felt like an earthquake, and we were at its epicentre. Dust flew and blanketed the atmosphere, choking the poor girl in the process. Even in death, the black and white family never stopped to hurt this poor girl. I didn't see it at first, but Opus raised her arm and pointed towards the clouded debris. What rolled along the defeated building was a cannon, and an army behind her. I could see the fear in Opus' eyes, as she looked towards the oncoming spawns of Hell.

I was absolutely livid at the demons for tormenting the pure little girl, to the point of her shaking when she saw her schoolmaster's face. I wanted to seek revenge, but I had to keep my mind clear, for I only sought to rescue her from Hell. We were at the end, but it made it all the more difficult to hold back my fury towards the black and white family. Mr Lonely was the one to seek revenge, but I was the one to rescue people and help them to their crows.

Alas, we were met face to face with our pursuer, and just like in my dreamscape, they never once looked at me, but instead, only at Opus. The schoolmaster looked at her with a more empty look than the railroad man, and only spoke the words,

"Come back; you're sick and unclean. You left in such a mess, and now you're **impure.**"

I couldn't help but shout, "Leave her alone, damn you! You've tortured her enough, and you've tortured me enough! May my mentor bless you with such forgiveness, for none of us will bless you with such." The white-cloaked figure said nothing; it didn't even seem like she heard me. She was truly only focused on Opus now; we were an impure lost cause.

I wanted to confront her with the deceit that she bestowed upon me, but she never even gave me the satisfaction of looking me in the eye. Without reconciling in what used to be azure orbs, I could only assume that they were scribbles now. The black and white family were driven to find power within others, and purify their imperfections; who was she to define health? I was enraged at the concept of her wanting to drag Opus to Hell, and "fix" what was necessary, but I finally understood why the crows gifted me with such an escape; it was to let Opus find hers as well. Although my job as her guide was complete, Mr Lonely's lust for revenge was just beginning.

It was unnerving to think that all of us understood the demons from Hell without an exchange of names, for we were all too familiar with their torment. Now it was time to end their reign among mindscapes, and it began with letting Opus free by the iron beast. Mr Lonely allowed one last intermission before the encore, but Opus never stepped forward. "I will carry coals no more, but fight for my freedom alongside foreign heroes. The dirt alongside my fingertips means nothing, if for the sake of pursuing dreams."

The schoolmaster in the white cloak sighed briefly, before she lit the first fuse.

"This world is in need of cleansing, and it would have brought great purity in knowing you were by my side, all of you. I gave you your gifts of pure power, and now you use them in imperfect ways."

She thought of herself as the reason for our gifts? She thought it was her who gave me my fire, and then sought to take it from me? I couldn't understand her anymore; I chose to never look at the woman before me as anyone else, other than a cold-hearted demon. In her ending phrase, a loud boom echoed, with the roar of her cannon signalling the beginning of the encore. The schoolmaster wanted unity in purity, but Opus wanted a freedom that earned hard labour. The railroad man wanted revenge for mockery, but I, Father Drexel, only wished for the great big moon in the sky to have a plan that involved a liberating movement. I beckon thee, one must always **chase their dreams until the end.**

The Encore

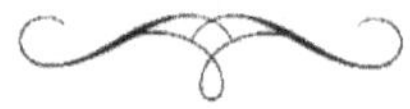

The schoolmaster led the charge towards us, paying no mind to the readying figure Mr Lonely bestowed. Even though my goal of saving the girl was complete, his goal of wanting revenge like no other had hardly just begun. I backed out of the way almost immediately, for he had already begun combat with cultists, and summoning trains. He cared nothing of the world around him, and saw the white cloaked figures as bowling pins. Shots were fired at us, and so I became the shield, and Mr Lonely the rapier.

Opus was the armour, for she was what the enemies aimed at, but never achieved a hit. The few that escaped the oncoming trains always charged towards the girl, but I never let them get past the ring of fire. I was utterly terrified of fighting the black and white family head-on, and was worried of my dreams truly predicting my future. Never wanting to risk it, I projected Hellfire onto each cloak, and sent them back to the debris of their home. I was able to keep a clean conscious within battle; the snow would save them from complete death, but their egos would never let them walk with burned skin. The schoolmaster fired cannonballs at only Mr Lonely now, seeing fit to come back to Opus, who was now behind me like a solar eclipse, once the railroad man was no longer in the picture.

The brief refuge in knowing Opus would be saved from focused attack was a relief, but still unnerving to know who it would be focused on now. I watched the railroad man look for something in the schoolmaster; was it the moment she lit the fuse, or was it something else? In a sudden wave of realisation, it came to me that he awaited for the schoolmaster to take a step further than her cannon. She never seemed to lift a single foot past the wheels of her own, but in the moment she did, I heard a distinct exclamation, "That's more like it, hoho!" Without a second to spare, Mr Lonely somersaulted and raised a train from the ground underneath him!

The schoolmaster being one foot away from her cannon was all that he needed to bring her up with him, without her weapon. The railroad man had successfully isolated them, and so the true battle had begun. I watched as they both fought with hand-to-hand combat, and the railroad man seemingly being victorious. However, the schoolmaster seemed to find a weakness that I never did: his mask. Any attack that the railroad man unleashed was quickly taken back to guard his mask.

In the heated moment, it looked as if the schoolmaster managed to trip Mr Lonely! He fell down, and seemed to slip off of the edge, but not without propelling himself back upwards. I was amazed at his ability to always turn his perils into an act, but it seemed as if his nerves were seeping through. He wanted his revenge already, and he wanted to end this. With another slip off of the top, coming back to a somersault, he landed with a new notion of rage.

The schoolmaster was growing in power, and managed to make Mr Lonely walk backwards. As he slowly walked to the edge of the last train cart, the schoolmaster simply flicked her fingers. It was hard to tell what she said in her last remarks, but the roar of her cannon being shot spoke volumes. The railroad man was hit, not necessarily his flesh, but his mask! I watched the hollowing white mask fall into the red snow, and all of the railroad man's former restraints.

He was no longer the balanced, charismatic, humming man he was. It was a monster exposed in light, and was ready to silence every ray. No one could see his face, but the fact alone that it was visible was enough to terrify everyone. He immediately charged towards the schoolmaster, grabbing her by the throat and jumping off of the locomotive. The brutal fight for survival hurt to watch, for the snow was no longer pure.

I turned to see if Opus was okay, but she was as distant as the black and white family. Although I tugged on her hand and wanted her to respond, she seemed to have left mentally to keep herself pure. Her absent mind reminded me of the fog I once lingered in during Hell. It pained me to see her in the fog, but I knew how comforting it was to see or feel nothing for a moment's while. I decided it would be best for the both of us to linger in the fog, and thus, I joined her in the bliss of mist. She turned to me in a spared moment, and spoke quietly. "Why does he only speak in song," she asked with a faint exhale. I didn't quite know what to think or say, so I only asked, "What do you mean?"

"I've had dreams of the tarrier, and he only spoke in songs of the railroad."

"Songs keep him working, I suppose. He'll find work, as long as he can find a song."

"And what is he without a voice?"

I looked to the railroad man for some sort of answer, but all I saw was a juggernaut of a monster against a demonic schoolmaster. Looking at the monster fight the schoolmaster was gut-wrenching, for it was a merciless bloodbath with gashes seemingly being from a direct result of its fingernails clawing into flesh. Mercy only seemed to come when he held her by the hair against the path of an oncoming train. I was bewildered by his lack of remorse, but knew I wasn't to judge a maskless, voiceless man.

When the inevitable crash of flesh meeting the iron beast was to happen, my eyes failed to see any sort of bloodshed, or anyone for that matter! The train was gone with a final exhale, and the man standing motionlessly in the snow. His back was towards both us and his mask, awaiting the presence of the schoolmaster once more. There were no cultists left, for many were crushed or scalded in snow. The dormant cannon that previously belonged to the schoolmaster was gone, and was only replaced by the demon from Hell that tormented me for years.

I was shocked to see the two transform into both of their points of nothing holding them back, to the point that human characteristics were no longer present. I watched the railroad man take slow, deliberate steps towards the tattered demon, with each hit of his boot making the sound of someone hammering a railroad spike. "You're not pure, and I'll be damned if you think killing a girl takes anything away. You can terrify anyone here, but not me. I know what you are, and it's nothing to be afraid of."

The tattered demon hissed at his words, but the railroad man paid no mind, as he walked closer.

"Just lay down your hammer and die, Lord, Lord."

The demon never seemed to give up, not until the railroad man shot them in the leg. He used the weapon of man against a creature from not of this world, and in an eye-widening defeat, the tattered demon hit the ground. To see such a figure I deemed immortally evil succumbing to the railroad man made me feel something I had yet to reconcile, yet I could only imagine what it was like for Opus as of now; her fog vanished with the defeat of Hell.

"A man without a voice is an ethic with nothing to aspire to."

"Would he be lost?"

"No, he'll find himself someway or another."

"Through song or through work?"

"Through neither, unfortunately; he has to find what caused him to lose his voice."

"And for the tarrier?"

"He lost his voice to a demon, and now the monster will die by his hammer."

"I thought demons could never die?"

"I thought so as well; we all did."

"Then how is this possible?"

"I guess your schoolmaster wasn't a demon, but simply fooled us into believing she was."

It was interesting to reconcile how she preyed on our vulnerabilities, to make us think of her as an immortal being. Our minds warped her into a flesh-consuming monster, when in reality, she was just a woman who preyed on impurities. Maybe the railroad man wasn't afraid of her in full, because he didn't see a tattered demon. Maybe Opus saw a different person than just her schoolmaster. Maybe I only saw her in similarities of the things around me, with the Cathedral of Flames making her look pure, my dreamscape making her look ghastly, and Hell making her look demonic. The Tower of Purity had crumbled, and Mr Lonely had readied a revolver pointed to its head.

"Whether you join the fabric of the universe, or burn in Hell, let everyone know that *this steel hammer drove you home.*"

With his final words being cast out into the sea of the stars, the single shot was fired into the demon's head. I felt the girl's body slightly jump from the sound, and watched in horror as she was ripped away from her bliss by the convulsing body before us. It was surreal to see the black and white family's demise in such a way, but alas, we made them up to be beings of a higher power, when they were just as imperfect as we were. They preyed on us in our worst moments, and caused dismay for moments without an end. The Man from Room #47 was never mad, but simply never joined the family. Like a sailor against the tides, it felt impossible to ride the storm out. It was only natural for the railroad man to sense the full picture, for he had more time to figure it out. Nevertheless, he knew where we came from, and he knew he wasn't too far ahead.

It was a mystery as to how the black and white family formed, where they originated from, and to whom they owed their purity to, but it was no secret that the schoolmaster was the leader. She was a toying traitor to the railroad man, a deceitful doctor to me, and a tormenting teacher to Opus, but to the black and white family, she was a saviour. She helped transform people to their purest form, never ceasing to stop until it was done. Her cult was lively, that was until we, the odd impurities, never chose to succumb to the void of colour. Now, we stood in the debris of everything she acclaimed, and the unfortunate followers as well.

We all watched the body seemingly fade with the sky, losing life with every breath, and with a final star shooting away from the great big moon in the sky, Mr Lonely turned his back to the corpse. The railroad man didn't turn to reveal his face, mock the dead, or offer any sort of appeasement, but only turned to retrieve his mask. When he approached us, I felt a sense of dread, never wanting to identify a single feature on his face. What I used to want to see like it was my final mission was now forbidden, and could be sentenced to death. However, it was inevitable to look at his rotten flesh when he knelt upon the snow to put his mask back on.

In the brief moments of his head lower than mine, I could see the way his skin was a discoloured, greenish grey. His flesh was rotting off in every crease, and sagging off of one of his eye sockets. There was not a single hair on his brow or chin, or even a lash on the one eyelid he still had. His eyes had no colour or iris, but only a dead gaze readying to be put under the mask once more. However, what I found most disturbing was his lack of a nose; there was only a hole leading to his skull, perfectly flat for his mask to cover.

Putting on his mask and hat, Mr Lonely acted as if we never saw his true flesh. Perhaps it was better that way, for the thought of the lengths he would go to hide it was silencing enough. Opus made a move before I did, and it was a move neither me nor the railroad man anticipated. She walked up to Mr Lonely, and hugged him. I couldn't think of anyone who would embrace a man who committed the acts he did a moment before, but to her, it meant more than either of us understood.

"Oh railroader, I thank you."

"What for?"

"For allowing me to speak. And you, Father Drexel. I thank you as well."

"What for?"

"For allowing me to see. They say that in our last moments, we only hear, but you, my friends, brought every sense back."

"Did you survive your last moments?"

"No, but it was worth each moment."

I thought back to the ceiling collapsing, and thought of the incoherent actions of Mr Lonely. It was only a wonder I had yet to notice sooner, for we became one and the same with our voices. I looked for any crow around us, but only saw debris, snow, and the moon. My mentor was proud of me, for I did all of what the moon asked: to save a soul. It seemed a part of Mr Lonely was saved as well, but in a more moral sense. He seemed to carry a goal bigger than mere revenge, and it was protection. Now that we had a young girl alongside our arms, the weight of choices grew stronger. Would it be the railroad man or the priest to continue her education? Would it be her to further our betterment? Would it be the locomotive to end the chapter?

With a final bow, Mr Lonely conjured a locomotive for all of us to board. I could see some sort of amusement with having a new passenger on board behind his mask, and the question stirring inside his hat whether she'll drink coffee or tea. The rumble of the ground shook all of us, and left us anticipating the stop of the iron beast. The head of the locomotive passed us, and with a train cart finally resting before us, Mr Lonely stepped upon the step and opened the door. "All aboard," he said with a hint of a smile. I beckon thee, one must always **look at their painting with a fresh pair of eyes.**

Fin

My dreams returned to a normal state, along with following the great big moon in the sky. I was at peace with myself and my mentor, and freely walked among the stars. On occasion, I could hear a faint train whistle or a piano medley, for I never strayed too far, even in a dreamscape. The past few years have been filled with wonder, from the girl's laughter to the railroad man's performances. We've taken turns helping Opus find her balance in character, and found that she is quite moving when provoked; even moving the objects around her.

Most mornings I am awakened by the train whistle, calling for me to prepare for the day. Outside was always a black void, but there was a beauty in it, after one's eyes were properly adjusted. The melodies of my mother tongue would sing softly on the radio, while I readied my person to enter the dining cart. It's always impossible to predict who will be the first to approach the table, but it was guaranteed to never be the railroad man. He only joined us once the smell of a fresh brew filled the air, whether it was me, Opus, or a mysterious notion to prepare it for him.

As for the girl's preference, she seemed to enjoy both. Between coffee with cream and a dash of vanilla, and black tea with orange and cinnamon, she crafted her own versions to enjoy the best of both. I will admit, she helped me develop a liking for coffee, but I could never favour it over tea. Mr Lonely seemed to enjoy the changes as well, but never switched from his black cup. Between mugs, cups, and glasses, it felt better knowing there was a way to use all three with both kinds of drinks.

On one day entering the dining cart, I could see Opus and Mr Lonely talking amongst each other. Talking was a poor choice of words, for they were singing a melody of sorts. *"Now listen to her rumble, now listen to her roar,"* the railroad man kept chanting. The girl would answer his calling, *"As she echoes down the valley, and flies along the shore."* I could hear the engine whistle, like a mighty call in response to all of us being united, as we rode the cars to somewhere **new.**

Mr Lonely no longer cared where the train seemed to take us; every stop was foreign, and it allowed a fortunate opportunity. On some mornings, we stopped in cities surrounded by water, while others were busy deserts. I trusted in the moon's placement for every journey, for the outcome always proved to be favourable. On the occasion that we ended up in a familiar place, such as Francia, Allemagne, or Russie, it never appeared to be melancholy without us. It was easy to tell we helped it break free of its own demons, and that it could now fully stand proud.

I hoped to **the great big moon in the sky** that Opus understood why the buildings were able to stand at full height, for her goal of wanting to perform for others would be impossible to reach without a full stand. Both Mr Lonely and I taught her many lessons using new terrain, with values of balance, and a voice. The railroad man would often take her to the outskirts of town, and take her through various courses to train her physicality, never failing to switch out of that ghastly monster of a man, once the lesson was completed to his standards. I would take her into town, following the crows and helping her kindle her own flame, which often meant helping her mentality. Through open cathedrals with spare pianos and abandoned train tracks, we were able to help Opus grow without depriving her of freedom.

It was hard to tell what Mr Lonely's plans for his future were, but one could tell that they weren't as mindlessly decided as before. His work melodies never ceased, but neither did his need for a better pair of trousers. While not having an end goal, he seemed to have an insatiable desire to improve. Only through the betterment of others did Mr Lonely ever find a value to take away. In the end, I hoped he would find reconciliation to put his mask on the dining cart table.

Thanks to my mentor above for seeing all that was in the world, I was blessed between the stars to have such a family. Between the balanced railroad man, and the hard-working musician, we seemed to always find purpose in each day. I had no doubt that if **the great big moon in the sky** called us all to another journey, we would be ready. All it would take was a simple change of dream, or even a mere change of weather. Until my mentor calls me, I will continue spreading the word of the crows and the trains to as many ears that would be willing to listen, and as many eyes that would be willing to read.

The girl that I grew to know and cherish formed her own person with each passing stop, with her sense of attire changing from the ball gown she wore, to a majorette-like uniform from Mr Lonely's time. It was a white jacket with a skirt built in, with blue trim and a small caplet hugging her. Although she wore a matching hat and a mask from her homeland, her locks of hair never ceased to stay the same. She truly resembled the perfect balance of the railroad man, herself, and me, and it was a true gift to cherish. I simply only hoped her consciousness never resonated with the railroad man's need to cover his face, for hers was still as pure as the undisturbed snow of the sleeping land.

The world is an ocean, with our fishing rods being our souls.

Where will we cast our line?

How far away are we willing to go?

The crows and the trains are like a compass. Where will we travel next, and where will you go?

I beckon thee, one must always **keep a compass.**

The Story Behind the Story

Who is *She?*

She was a fifteen year old girl at the time of writing. However, her passion for writing has extended throughout almost her entire life! From fictitious adventures with her friends to early concepts of novels she'd later publish, she grew as a writer exponentially. In spare time, she writes poetry and draws pictures of her loved ones. In time, what she valued would grow to influence her stories.

Who is Mr. Lonely?

Mr. Lonely is a man of the railroad, but he wasn't always the train-enthusiastic German people know him to be. When *she* was only eleven years old, she created a lost book consisting of a woman inheriting a family manor, and a ghastly figure named Mr. Lonely as well. Through the help of other family spirits, Mr. Lonely would supposedly be defeated. However, due to the pandemic, the documents were lost within *her* old school. Almost four years later, *she* brought him back with newly found inspiration from old train songs.

Who is Father Drexel?

Father Drexel is a man of the great big moon in the sky. While inspired by many religious figures in *her* life, he is mainly derived from *her* family history. The name "Drexel" was a family name on *her* mother's side, and his appearance is in relation to *her* father's fraternal organisations. As for his story, it was based off of an unfinished novel *she* wrote that consisted of a travelling plague doctor who cured people through mysterious power. In time, he grew to become the personification of a newly found faith.

Who is Opus?

Opus is a young girl who loves music, and values creativity over rationality. Throughout the early stages of the book, her character was mostly without a finish. She was originally going to be a ghost that helped the travelling plague doctor, who he previously failed to save. At other times, she would be a boy, who would act as a messenger between the railroad man and the father. Nevertheless, her character stayed as a young girl, inspired by a childhood book, and a porcelain doll *she* once saw in a retirement home.

Who is the Schoolmaster?

The Schoolmaster was a peculiar woman with values of purity and control. In *her* opinion, the woman's story is the most interesting. The schoolmaster's black and white family was inspired by *her* encounters with an actual cult, and *her* family's history with them as well. The white-cloaked figure's powers would remain uncertain during early stages of planning, until *she* asked one of her loved ones to name something powerful. As for the whole family's ethnicity and design, it was heavily inspired by one of *her* favourite songs that was famously known for both their Russian and English versions

Closing Remarks.

If one starts with the earliest concept of a character, then it took *her* four years to write this book.

If one starts with the earliest concept of the book, then it took *her* two years to write this book.

If one starts with the earliest time of a completed plot, then it took *her* only a year to write this book.

If one starts with a feeling of no motivation, the outcome will never feel fulfilled or satisfied.

If one starts with a feeling of ease and a thought out plan, the outcome will bring the utmost favour.

Hold on to those dreams, and let them breathe.